WRONG SIDE
OF THE ROAD

Sam Boatwright

Grosvenor House
Publishing Limited

This book is published by
Grosvenor House Publishing Ltd
Link House
140 The Broadway, Tolworth, Surrey, KT6 7HT.
www.grosvenorhousepublishing.co.uk

A CIP record for this book
is available from the British Library

ISBN 978-1-78623-201-4

To my brothers and my best friends, Matthew and Luke,
I run to make you proud.

To Kerry, my wife, our challenge is just getting started,
and I can't wait.

Thank You

Without some incredibly important people I would have never made it across and for your help and love, I thank you. If I have missed you out I can only apologise:

To Mum and Dad, I have no idea why I am able to run like I can, or sit on a bike for as long as I can but I am sure whatever that little part of me that is drive and determination, it comes from you two.

To my brilliant 'Epic Adventure' Team, I cannot thank you enough. You gave up your time and your holidays to make sure I made it across. You laughed with me and you cried with me and you were there when I needed you.

To Anthony Hannan, your wit and intelligence make me want to take you on every adventure with me. We have spent more time in close proximity than two friends should ever have to but you never fail to make me laugh. You sacrificed having your daily shower and you even cleaned the toilet pipe - a true gentleman.

To Matthew Wright, you were there every time I needed your navigation skills, finding roads I don't think 'Google' even knew existed, you are a prince among men and a brilliant human being.

To Helen and Darren Foster, I only hope that Kerry and I are as happy as you two, a more wonderful couple you will not meet. You guys stuck with me in the darkest moments, when the roads tested me and quitting was the easy way out. You guys are grit, determination and happiness personified.

To Saj Hussain, it seems like a lifetime ago that I was sat telling you my ideas about America. Without you that's what they would be – ideas. Thank you.

To my (now) wife, Kerry, everyone told us how hard a test it would be, how much we would argue and fall out. We made it, and we made it all the way to Vegas. It was definitely easier to finish knowing I was coming back to begin married life with you. I love you without rhyme or reason, and I look forward to all the challenges to come with you by my side.

To my little brother, Luke, for your editing skills and for permanently correcting my spelling and grammar.

To my eldest brother, Matthew (Trev), for answering the phone whenever I call.

Thank you to Sion and Shelley, I hope to one day repay the favour.

Thank you to every single person that wrote me a message, shared my page, retweeted a tweet, donated to charity, bought us a hotel room or even let us stay with you for a night - you helped me to make the impossible possible and to inspire the uninspired.

Contents

Chapter 1

Prologue

April 6th 2012. Blackpool.....

Blackpool was cold and unbelievably grim that morning. I will never forget the smell, adrenaline, fear and overwhelming feeling of dread. What the heck was I doing? Who the hell did I think I was? I had never run a marathon, let alone 50 miles. I was about to run 2,500 miles around the UK mainland, 50 miles every day for 50 days. And why....why? I don't think I have an answer to this, even now. Was it an escape from the life I had created? Was I trying to run away from the problems I had made at home? Was I really going to try and run all of these miles? Whatever the reason was, I was off. One foot in front of the other for 50 miles.

The run took me all around the UK mainland, places I had never seen. From Blackpool I pushed North to Carnforth and up the coast to Scotland. Scotland is beautiful, majestic, enchanting and amazingly unforgiving. People are rare in Scotland, there is more wildlife than people. At first this is great, freedom from the norm, after a while the solitude takes hold. It is the solitude that slowly starts to hurt your mind. Pain eats at you in a completely different way. The feeling of overcoming pain is a triumphant feeling, you feel like you have won. The mind, however, is a different beast entirely. It can bog you down for days, months or even years at a time. Trauma or change can make you a different person. Scotland changed me, it broke me down.

A climb called 'Rest and Be Thankful' was one of the toughest days on the run. 7 miles of climbing, stretching out to the heavens, a never-ending path of pain. Much like with any vicious climb in Scotland the view at the top was breath-taking and (quite possibly) worth the tortuous ascent. Throughout Scotland, it has to be said, that I cursed myself for having never seen more of this amazing country. Beautiful lochs, peaceful and still, almost prehistoric, like each one has its own story to tell – it is an awe-inspiring place and one which I can only encourage people to go and visit.

I ran out of Fort William on one of the coldest days on the run. As I ran, it began to snow. The snow only made me fight harder to keep moving, another challenge for me to overcome. If I was to break it certainly wouldn't be the weather that would do it. The snow accumulated on the brow of my hat, building up like a mini snow drift. I crested yet another climb, as I did I saw the monument to our fallen marines. I stood and stared at it for a while, a stark reminder of why I was running. "You run for those that can't!" I told myself and with that I plodded onwards.

I arrived in Elgin, my most northerly point. A quaint little town where we were told we would be lucky to find a room. It was a wet Wednesday in April, we found a room.

Any time you turn a corner and head in a different direction on a run you feel some sense of accomplishment, as of now I would be heading South and back towards England. I began to descend Scotland, firstly through Aberdeen and then into Edinburgh. Much of the running in Edinburgh followed the path of the official Edinburgh marathon. I weaved my way through the narrow busy streets always working back towards England. Entering England on St George's day was fantastic, a real sense of patriotism filled my veins and I plundered heartily through the miles down the North East coast.

All around the coast of Britain you see spectacular scenery and meet some wonderful people. Running didn't just teach me about what my body would take. It opened my eyes to how fantastic our tiny island is and also to how brilliant the people who inhabit it are. The saying goes 'never judge a book by its cover'. This was never truer for me than on one day in Newcastle. I had stopped for a quick bite to eat, weary and tired the weather had battered me all day. I was not looking for conversation. A young man walked towards me, wearing a baseball cap, and a hoodie - his hood pulled up over his hat, covering his face. Adidas tracksuit bottoms with bright white trainers and pearly white socks beaming out. Here stood a 'chav', in every understanding and definition of the word. His walk was typically more of a gangster shuffle than an actual walk – I was terrified. I could feel my body brace and tense up as he approached, expecting my phone or watch to be stolen. Instead, in a thick Geordie accent he said -

"You're that bloke who is running?"

(My jaw must have nearly broken my toes. How the heck did he know what I was doing?)

"Yes, yes, I am," I replied in complete shock.

"Here you are pal."

He handed me some money. I was speechless.

He had just donated to 'Help for Heroes'. Wow. I cursed myself for judging him. I am still to this day astounded by his donation. This young man taught me a valuable lesson and made me see that people could be brought together over something that they believe in. I ran through some of the most deprived areas of Britain and all I saw was generosity and the kindness of strangers.

The East coast of England gave me some of the toughest weather conditions on the run. A bruising barrage of rain, sleet, wind and snow hammered against my body, unrelenting in its attempt to break me. Along the coast we went, Whitby, Bridlington, Filey, Skegness - we passed many seaside towns, some benefitting from recent investment, others in need of a great deal of help.

One of my favourite places on the trip down the East Coast was Cromer. A beautiful, elegant town where time seems to have stood still. The large buildings look to be from the 1920s. We stayed in a large country house in Cromer; there was no charge for the room, the owners just wanted to help. A free standing bath sat in the middle of the bedroom and I remember thinking how quiet it was. No hum of traffic or sirens blaring out, just complete tranquillity. When I set off the following day I ran passed the beach huts as I continued down the coast. All the huts were different colours, immaculately preserved, a real beach of British history and tradition.

It is strange how much of certain parts of the first run I still remember and the bits that I can't remember, as well. Much of the East coast seems to blur into one or two days when in reality it took me over a week. Just like in Elgin when I turned and ran south my goal was now Dover and to turn and run West, a new wind direction, another coast.

I arrived in Dover on a typically British day. It had rained a little in the morning, the sun had come out for about 11 minutes and then it had rained again. Couldn't get a much more British day? I had only ever come through Dover on a school trip to Euro Disney and so had never paid much attention to it. Dover is grim. The only thought going through my head was, "Wow, when people seek asylum in Britain they must get here and think, oh God what have we done?" Years of weathering have taken its toll on Dover, it has been beaten to its knees and is struggling to get up. We looked around for places to stay in Dover but stayed towards the outside of the town. As much as possible, I wanted to see or do the iconic tourist things on our coastline. The White Cliffs of Dover are a huge part of British history. I stood on top of the cliffs for quite some time, looking out over the channel towards France. It is just over 20 miles to France from Dover. I could be there and back in a day I thought. I knew I was close to France, as when I looked at my phone my service provider flicked from French to English and back again.

The south coast of England is a stunning place filled with dazzling beaches and charming towns. From the top to the bottom of the UK, there is a stark contrast. Each town, each place has its own way of selling itself, each destination a tiny bit different from the last. Scotland's beaches are wild, untrodden and bleak. The south coast is more managed and tamed with houses sprinkled all along the cliff edges.

Running on the south coast saw some of the harder days on the run. I don't know whether it was my mind or my terrible lack of knowledge of the south coast but some of the climbs down there were brutal. It was up and down every day. Lynmouth, still to this day, stands out as one of my toughest days, a 25% gradient heading into the town and a 25% gradient heading out. It was a climb that never seemed to end. Heading out of the town was soul destroying. It was painfully warm and even the support vehicle was straining under the pressure of the gradient. Every step I took, the camper van groaned and creaked its way forward, the boys in the support crew honking the horn and cheering just to try and keep me moving. On any climb I have the same philosophy, put your head down and count to 50, don't look up - ever. On this climb it was impossible not to look up, at some points the gradient was so steep I could lean forward and touch the tarmac. My slow running pace had dropped even more; I was only just above a walk by this point. The hill climbed for two and a half miles, with the sun beating down on my back. Sweat poured from me, staining the road as I passed. Step by step, I was slowly edging my way up the hill. It is an awful feeling to seemingly be aware of the life draining out of you, to feel your body empty; with every drop of sweat more energy was leaving my body. My lungs heaved hard for more air, I just couldn't take in enough air to satiate the amount of oxygen my body needed. Finally, and mercifully I reached the peak, brutal yet triumphant I stood at the top, a part of me left forever on the ascent.

The south coast not only saw the toughest climb but it also was the scene of my hardest, loneliest day. A massive amount of planning goes into any challenge. The Epic Run was particularly difficult logistically as I was dependent on a whole team of people to be in certain places at certain times. Some of these people I had never met or were people I barely knew. However, all of them played their own part in ensuring I finished the run.

While I was on the south coast one of my drivers had to return to work, the next driver would not arrive until the day after, meaning I had one day with no driver at all. I remember sitting and pondering for a long time what I should do, who I should call. I had already been helped by one of my Twitter followers who had come to my aid after a mayday call across a multitude of social networks. This time I was struggling. My home town is a good 8 hour drive from the south coast and with many people already putting in a massive effort to help me get around, I needed to do something different, I also knew I couldn't put anything on social media this time or I would panic my family.

The plan was very simple. I would wake up as early as I could in the morning (I was aiming for 4am). I would run the first stretch which would be about 15 miles and then somehow get back to the camper van and then I would drive myself the 15 miles I had just run. I would repeat this throughout the day, what a great plan I thought. The only problem with a 4am start is you force a lack of sleep on an already depleted body, not to mention it's dark, damp and thoroughly unenjoyable. I ran the first 15 miles; it was hard, not hard like some other days where the gradient was hard, this was hard because I was alone. I couldn't stop and sit down; there was no chatting or horn beeping to keep me going.

This was isolation, loneliness and a solitude worse than that I had experienced in Scotland. It made me appreciate enormously the people who had given up their time to come and drive for me, the sacrifices they had made to make sure I made it. And, so it went, like a caterpillar all day. 10 miles, 5 miles or 15 miles I would run in sections and then get the public bus back to where I had left the camper van with everyone at home completely oblivious to what I was doing. I still remember now getting the bus, I hadn't shaved since the beginning of the run and I was now about 6 weeks in. It was quite cold so I was wearing my hat. I was dressed in running tights and a thick long sleeved top. I don't imagine I was what most people expected on the first bus of the day. Thoroughly bedraggled, tired and lonely I sat on the bus and rested my head against the window, I stared at nothing, I couldn't tell you anything I passed that day on the bus, a blur of colour. Each bus trip back all I could think to myself was, "I've just run this." The bus journey seemed to be over in minutes whereas the run seemed to take forever. After 19 hours of moving, my day was done. I slept.

Arriving at Land's End was a great feeling but also somewhat of an anti-climax. For many Land's End is the end of their challenge or the start of one if they are going the other way. For me, it was a milestone, another little landmark ticked off my list. I remember being stood next to the sign at Land's End; it has loads of different places pointed out with their mileage. The first thing I looked at was how far away John O'Groats was, the second one was how far away New York was. Both challenges I would undertake in the following years. After the obligatory pictures, I began running North, I remember thinking, I am running home.

For me, the north is home. It is different up north. If you are from the south and have never been north you should go and vice versa. There is something quite unique about the people in northern Britain. They are harder, not in a way that I mean they can beat everyone up. I mean they are weathered; they have what I call "Northern Grit". We are used to the dank, horrible weather, we are used to the dark, cold nights, and we are used to be being the underdog. Northerners have a certain way, a way of getting things done. It's the grit, steel and sheer bloody-mindedness of people from the north that enables me to do what I do.

I knew once I got into Wales it was the last push, the last bit of my journey. I was almost home. From the south coast I would push north up to Bristol and then across the Severn Bridge and into Cardiff. Just to give any readers a quick heads up you are not supposed to run across the Severn Bridge. Once they spot you running across it, they are pretty quick to let you know that it's not allowed.

Wales was everything I hoped it would be and I can see why the Welsh are so proud of their country. I remember running with rolling hills on one side of me and the sea on the other side. I don't think I have a favourite place in the world as there have been so many amazing places but I think Barmouth has to be very close. Barmouth sits on the edge of the Snowdonia National Park, south of Porthmadog and north of Aberystwyth. A more beautiful place you will struggle to see. I ran slowly through, trying my hardest to take everything in. A tiny piece of heaven on the coast of Wales, tucked away, completely untouched by the masses.

It had rained almost every day since departing from Blackpool but Wales gave me something else. It gave me sunshine, glorious, glorious sunshine. No matter where you are in the world if the weather is awful it makes enjoyment that little bit tougher, now the sun was out and the smile on my face was not going away. I was now running through Snowdonia National park, for the first time in 7 weeks I had come away from the coast and was heading in land towards my home town of Skipton. The majestic scenery in Wales kept my mind busy as I bounced my way through the hills and homeward.

Chapter 2

The Aftermath

A lot can happen in 5 years. When I finished the Epic Run, I felt invincible. It was a strange time and a strange feeling for me. It felt like I could do anything, I could conquer anything. Everything was going well. Strangely and slowly, however, my world started to implode. I started to implode.

For the previous 18 months all my focus had been on the run. Mile after mile of constant, mind numbing running whether on the road or preparing to be on it. Looking back now that's the only way I feel I can describe how I was. My mind was numb. The decisions I made were ridiculous, bordering on insane. I didn't even recognise myself. This was not a man I was proud of at all.

I dedicated my last book to my parents. The people that made me who I am today. They must have struggled so hard during those weeks, months and possibly years after the run. I think I must have been a hard person to be proud of, as I hurt so many people in the aftermath of that run. I won't name you, but all I can do is say sorry. It changes nothing but it allows me to say it.

May 26th 2012

I had done it. I had completed the challenge that everyone told me was impossible. I had run 2,500 miles around the UK mainland and I had done the entire thing in 50 days and with a smile (or at least an attempt at a smile) on my face. I remember lying in bed that night and just thinking, "What next?" Offers from all over the place came in for me to go run with people, to see what I could put my body through again. All I wanted to do was sit down and do nothing for a while. It's a strange feeling - to feel lost, to feel useless. I know you will read this and think how can a person who has just done 2,500 miles feel useless but that's exactly how I felt. I had no purpose anymore. No reason to get up and put my socks on, life was, well, life was 'normal' again. There came a point about 3 weeks after the run. I call this, the bottom. I was giving motivational speeches in schools, giving out awards, opening buildings, signing autographs, all the while fighting 'The Black Dog'. It's a fight many have had, there is never a winner. It's the first time in my life where I felt like I had nowhere to turn. I remember so clearly the message I sent to my mum. I can only imagine what she must have felt, watching her son break.

TEXT:

ME: I'm having dark thoughts mum. Don't know what to do anymore.

As always, as mothers so often do, her reply made me smile. So simple....

MUM: You don't need to have dark thoughts, we care.

To feel lost is one thing, to feel alone is far, far worse, I wasn't alone.

To the outside world everything seems fine, you look fine (although weight fluctuates), and you can function normally but inside you're screaming. It affected everything I did after the run, all the people I knew suffered because I was suffering.

It's taken me 4 years to put the run to bed. To move past it, to get back to being me again.

Like anything in life, it was a battle, hard work and something I had to work incredibly hard to beat. I'm not sure I would call it depression. I have spoken to people who suffer with this and I'm not sure I felt the same way that they do. I felt more like every decision I made was wrong, or maybe the decisions I made were not ones that I would have normally made. I could get up every morning and I could go to work. My problem was I didn't know where I was supposed to fit in, what I was supposed to do now.

I then began to blame everyone else for things I did and the decisions I made. I blamed everyone but myself. In the cold light of day and with the help of hindsight, what I was doing was sociopathic; I was telling people what they wanted to hear, I was lying to the people I loved and cared about in order to try and make them happy. It was a way for me to not deal with everyday things, not to have to deal with confrontation or make decisions I didn't want to have to make.

Once the low point has been hit and you are at the bottom it's much easier in a way, there is nowhere else to go but up. I make it sound like these things happened over a few weeks or months, when in fact this was the next three years of my life. It wasn't until my 32nd birthday when I was sitting at home after another relationship had broken down that I knew I needed to sort myself out. I wasn't about to check myself into rehab or anything like that but I knew I needed to sort myself out before anyone else got hurt or before I plunged deeper into despair.

I knew (and still know) only one way to sort myself out - I kicked my own ass, and this time I did it properly. The running shoes came out and off I went. I had a job I loved, I had my health, my family, my friends and my house, everything else would take time but I would get there.

Chapter 3

Finding Failure

I am often told that I am too harsh, too brutal in terms of my opinion. Firstly, it is exactly that, an opinion and one that I am entitled to. Secondly, and most importantly, we have become a society of wimps, a society of people who cannot take criticism. If I am too brutal, too honest about someone's abilities, I am twice as brutal and honest about my own abilities. The thing that most people can't deal with is the truth.

Like anyone I find failure hard to take, I think it is likely that you are going to find life very difficult. Even though emotionally I was a broken man, my physical prowess from the run still had me on top athletically. I was Rocky, I was Batman...hell, I was flipping Superman! I was taking on challenge after challenge, continuing to push my body. Maybe not akin to 2,500 miles of running over 50 days but I was certainly still pushing myself. I was channelling everything I had into my body, then came the JOGLE. A new challenge and a new discipline - a bike.

The current record from John O'Groats to Land's End stands at 41 hours, 4 minutes and 22 seconds. This route is 874 miles and the most direct road from the top of the UK to the bottom. The record is set on a push bike. It wasn't like I didn't train, every day, 2-3 hours. Sacrificing everything to get on the bike, to get in the gym. I gave the attempt everything I had.

It broke me in a way that even now hurts to write about. I was confident I could do it. I sat on the start line, like any other challenge completely convinced I had done the hard work in training. What I did not account for and where more research should have been done was the wind. What a little so-and-so a head wind is. When you run, a head wind is a pain but it has to be incredibly forceful to really put you off your stride, on the bike I felt like I was holding a sail above my head. The harder I pushed the slower I felt. I was in a standing attack to go downhill, powering the pedals in order to just keep moving.

I had never thought about what it would feel like to fail. It was awful, a strange empty feeling that I had never felt before nor do I ever want to feel again. Pushing out of John O'Groats I instantly knew how hard this challenge would be. The previous 48 hours had been a nightmare. Drivers I had lined up to help me pulled out at the last minute or couldn't make the journey there. I headed to Scotland with my Dad and another driver Tom, a friend from school. What I put them through and what they saw happen I can't imagine was pleasant. They saw me break, they watched me be destroyed by the weather and by the challenge I was attempting.

The strange thing about the JOGLE attempt is that I can't remember specific details about it, I can't remember what the towns were called or where the breathtaking landscapes were. When you conquer something the pain and suffering it took to get their pales into insignificance in contrast to the achievement, when you fail at something the bits you did wrong are magnified and eat at you forever.

We didn't arrive into John O'Groats until late on the evening before the attempt, a windswept hotel with a small bar downstairs. We threw our bags in hungry and tired. We descended the stairs into a bar, one local man clutching a pint stood at the bar. No food was served after 9pm the bar staff politely told us and we wouldn't be able to get breakfast until after 7.30am. I needed to leave at 5am. A few Mars Bars and peanuts were bought to try and ease the hunger a little. We adjourned to our beds, already deflated.

As I lay in bed that night the wind battered the sky light above my head, rain pelted the windows, it was a long and very loud night. We headed to the start point that morning, the mini bus swayed in the wind. The type of day where high-sided vehicles are not allowed to cross bridges and parts of trees lay strewn across the road. The three of us stood at the sign post at John O'Groats to take photos, unable to talk properly as the wind stole our words. I sat on the bike. I had done the hard work. I gave it everything I had. I emptied every energy reserve in my body, it wasn't enough.

My lasting memory is a picture of my sitting on the side of the road. It's dark, the mini bus lights are on me, head down, I'm beaten. I look at the picture sometimes even now, it's hard to look at but it also makes me remember that I have been down. I have been beaten, I have failed, but I have learnt from my failure.

A broken man. JOGLE attempt August 2015.

Chapter 4

America. The Land Of...

I am an ideas man. I think my dream job would be to work for a business where I just come up with new business ideas. I love it – embracing my creative side. For me, though, the ideas always revolve around what I could possibly push my body to do next. The following are the 3 questions that I constantly ask myself when I come up with an initial idea:

1. Is it hard enough to be called a challenge?
2. Am I likely to get shot while I am there?
3. Will I have to sleep in a tent?

I don't consider things like cost or whether I might die completing the challenge. I err on the side of possibility which usually requires a small step away from what most like to call the 'real-world'.

America for any adventurer (I guess that's what I call myself now) is a place full of intrigue. It's not an unknown quantity, we know what's there, however, for me as a little islander, a person brought up in a village of around 3 surnames, America is the great unknown.

I realise now how explorers must have felt throughout history, it's exactly how I felt when I first had the idea. I saw it as the 'land of opportunity', a land of great appeal. After spending 6 weeks there I now know that whatever your adventure is, you can find it in America. I believe that there is a paramount reason that so few Americans choose to travel overseas, it's not because they don't want to or because they don't like anyone else, it's more because.....why would you? When you have every type of holiday and climate that you could want in one country, why leave?

I remember thinking when we were in New York how every stereotype of America was real. Those in New York were loud, brash and somewhat arrogant but what I realised about America was that they didn't take it as an insult, instead they embraced their stereo-types. The hillbillies were hillbillies, so much so that when we went through one town, they even had a café called "Hill Billy Café". In Texas and Oklahoma, we met some red-necks, that's exactly what they had, red necks. I recall staring at a man in utter disbelief at what I was looking at!

One stereotype that bothered me somewhat was that of Americans being obese. When people mentioned to me about the size of some people in the US, I always just laughed it off thinking that I had seen overweight people before. Well, an overweight person in England looks like a cocktail stick compared to some of the people in America. It's pretty sad to see to be honest. People don't walk anywhere and with my experience of the roads out there, I can understand why, especially in the big cities. From time to time the pavement would just end whilst I was running on it, no warning. I would be running along and then - BAM - no pavement and I am in the middle of the road. Now don't get me wrong this isn't the sole cause of the weight epidemic in the good, old US of A but it doesn't help if you are risking your life just by walking to the corner shop!

America's allure and my somewhat obsessive fascination with the iconic Route 66, provided all the reason I needed to at least want to give this challenge a try. I still remember on the first Epic Run a friend saying to me, "Whatever the human mind can conceive it can achieve!" I love that saying; it makes me believe that anything is possible. This is also what I love about America and for that matter Americans in general, they have a belief in themselves, a belief that they can achieve greatness – that they will attain the 'American Dream' no matter wat. How could this ever be a bad thing?

Chapter 5

New York

"What a thoroughly miserable day!" This is what I thought to myself as I loaded my pack and headed for the start line. The start line was an imaginary one that went across Times Square. I wanted somewhere iconic and memorable. I certainly got that. The team and I had spent the previous 48 hours attempting to get our bearings around this concrete jungle of a city. New York oozes cool from every corner. The coffee shops are not just some little pantry that your granny goes too, they are chic boutiques that sell wheat grass incensed with camel urine. Each coffee shop is trying to outdo the others in their race to be the next great place. For me, I just want to sit down and drink a coffee. Simple. Maybe that's the miserable Yorkshireman in me, I don't know, but whatever "it" is, New York has "it" and it has "it" by the bucket load.

Craning your neck up as you navigate the city you get a real sense of how massive this city really is. Not just by surface area but as the skyscrapers tower above you, you feel dwarfed and unbelievably inconsequential. They drive out of the Earth like an alien form, shuddering and barging their way to the heavens. We all did touristy stuff while in New York, taking in as much as possible but we barely scratched the surface. I am not a city boy, in fact quite the opposite, but New York is different. It sucks you in, like a good book it leaves you wanting more. You need to see what is round the next corner because it could be the Flat Iron, the Empire State Building, Rockefeller Centre, Brooklyn Bridge or even the Statue of Liberty and even after seeing all of these, you have barely scratched the surface.

New York is every stereotype you have ever heard about America. Everything is massive; the people, the buildings, the food and the personalities. They are huge, larger than life, but not to see it and just to believe what people tell you is a huge mistake. Yes, they are big and brash but my God are they brilliant. New Yorkers have an air of confidence that is almost arrogant and yet, at the heart of it, they are truly warm and wonderful people who want nothing more than for you to see New York for what it is, a festival of culture. New York is an eclectic mix of languages, races and religions. On every corner, there will be a street vendor selling, performing or even just standing completely still.

As we traversed the streets of New York, I couldn't help but notice how amazingly warm it was. We had arrived into JFK late on the Saturday afternoon. Jeans were not my greatest choice of travel attire and I stood outside the airport and sweated while we hailed a taxi. As I think now of the sweat trickling down my back and my jeans sticking to me in a way that made me feel like I was suffocating, I realise that this moment was a miniscule prelude to the heat and discomfort that I would experience for the vast majority of my six weeks in America. I remember vividly feeling scared at this moment, the challenge was very real as we stood waiting for that taxi, very real.

It was early on the 24th of July 2017, I was in New York City, New York, America and I was already soaked. I had made the decision earlier in the planning to run to the bottom of Manhattan Island and then cross over the bridge. Now, those that have been to New York will know that there is no such bridge. This became all too apparent after I was staring at the Statue of Liberty wondering how the heck I could have been quite so stupid. I can understand the odd wrong turn during the 3,000 miles but I had only done 8 miles, I was drenched and already I had run in the wrong direction! To anyone who saw me or maybe more to the point heard me that morning I apologise, my language was somewhat choice. I stood for a good five minutes, holding back tears but also with a little smile on my face. "Sam, you plonker!" I said it to myself many more times on the trip, always trying to sound like Del Boy off of Only Fools and Horses.

After a swift about turn I headed back up Manhattan, hugging the water's edge towards The George Washington Bridge. The bridge loomed far in the distance quite often engulfed by the mist of the early morning drizzle. The skyscrapers that are normally the skyline of the city were shrouded by cloud that morning. Only half of Tower One was visible from the ground and the rest were cloaked in an eerie smog. As much as I cursed myself for going so badly wrong I also loved seeing downtown again. The rest of Manhattan passed without incident, runners passed and cyclists whipped by, no pleasantries were made just people going about their daily lives. They probably weren't even aware of my wry smile. As they each passed they had no clue that I was running for any other reason than they were, however, 32 days later I would be in LA in the baking sun.

As I arrived at The George Washington Bridge I was immediately struck by the enormity of it. This huge iron beast spanning the water. Getting onto the bridge as a pedestrian is no mean feat! Small streets, crossing large roads until finally your feet hit the mesh on the iron bridge. The water below a dark, mucky colour, looks lifeless. "There wouldn't be much of you left if you fell in!" I thought to myself as I slid my feet carefully across the bridge. Vertigo kicked in, If I haven't already mentioned, I hate heights, hate them. I was actually debating as to whether to get flat on my stomach and commando crawl across the bridge when the heavens opened (a little more). "Sod this!" I thought as I powered over the bridge and on towards New Jersey.

The team had already headed to New Jersey to collect the RV. The RV was a mystery, we had booked it and we knew it was pretty big but that was about it. We could have a collected a shed-on wheels or some 2-bed minivan, instead what we got was luxury on wheels. OK, maybe not 5-star luxury but it was pretty amazing. Firstly, I am six feet three inches tall and I could stand up in it. Secondly, I could have a poo in it and my legs were not round my ears while I was sat on the toilet and thirdly it had air conditioning (or something they called air-conditioning in the brochure). Our mobile home was ready, 5 weeks of luxury.....?

We had made the decision to communicate with short-wave radio. In planning, this was a great idea, the team would never be too far away and I could be navigated through the streets by them as they went ahead. As with many plans on this adventure, it didn't quite go as expected. The radio waves were filled with truckers, nannies, emergency services or they were out of range. I stopped outside a house not really paying much attention to who was round me:

"Hey dude, you got the time?" the voice said with a gangster-like rasp to his voice. As I looked up from screaming at my now pointless but apparently much needed radio, I saw what can only be described as a gang in front of me. Maybe they preferred the title posse or crew, whichever it was, I was currently on their turf and I was complete unaware of it – until right this second. Not only that but I did not exactly blend in, I was definitely the only tall, ginger, white bloke in the area and even worse I am unquestionably English and I was dressed head to toe in Lycra. As with many things in America your eyes are drawn to the differences, and the differences for British people are the guns. These fine young gentlemen must have been members of a gun club or some other fine community help group as many of the seemed to be quite heavily armed. I squeezed the broken radio hard in my hand, cursing the stupid decision not to buy an American SIM card. A thousand different thoughts were running through my mind, "I can't die here," I thought, "I haven't even managed one day!" Wow, how profound! Once my mind had calmed, I was able to swallow the sick that had appeared in my throat and quickly check my underwear to make sure I had not unconsciously sent out a brown alert. I then managed to muster in the most pre-pubescent voice imaginable a - "No, I'm fine thanks". I didn't even answer the original question but I didn't care. I was gone, a blur of black and ginger speeding through the streets! My calls on the radio were no longer calm, pleasant calls, now it was, "COME IN, HELP! HELP! HELP!!!" Eventually, the mayday calls were answered, the team had tracked me via my GPS tracker.

The first leg on the journey was a 96-mile slog down to Philadelphia via New Jersey. Once I had met up with the rest of the team, I collected my bike and caught some of the mileage up that I had lost while taking the scenic route around New York. It was hard for the RV to stay close to me in the city as the traffic was manic and we became somewhat of a hazard. The rain as it had done all day lashed me and beat me, trying its hardest to defeat me. I had been moving for 15 hours when a car pulled out in front of me at a junction. As the car pulled out, lightning clattered a lamp post near by producing a deafening crack - I was done for the day. I rolled into a retail car park, tail between my legs, desolate and at that moment the most alone I had ever felt. An alien in New York.

Day 1, Setting of from New York, Times Square.

Chapter 6

Yo Adrian

Philadelphia is known as the 'City of Brotherly Love', I can completely see why. Its quiet pavements and big wide roads make it easy to travel around with little chance of bumping into each other. It's laid back, so much so that the thought of running or cycling really didn't appeal to me. At times, I just wanted to sit down and chat with the guys.

Any challenge I take on I try to make sure that I am the underdog, I kind of enjoy thinking that people might bet against me. One thing I have found very hard since completing the Epic Run round the UK was that people didn't doubt, in fact quite the opposite, they expected me to succeed. With success comes expectation, expectation brings with it pressure. It seems stupid really, there was no pressure at all but my mind would not let me believe this. My mind created its own pressure, its own expectation.

I stared at the steps and the statue for a while. The greatest underdog story of all time? I had watched the most recent instalment of this story not long before I had left, the underdog once again creating history, inspiring people - pure hope. As a team we ran up the steps, the previous days beating had meant ascending the stairs was not the most pleasant of experiences but one I was determined to complete. When planning this adventure, the "Rocky Steps" were right at the top of the list of things I wanted to do. This is mainly apparent because Philadelphia was well out of our way, we could have just set off from New York and headed west towards Chicago and saved ourselves a lot of time and what was to become some serious pain on the bike but I needed my Rocky fix. From Rocky in 1979 to present day he has overcome pain and adversity - battling, dreaming and believing in himself. I feel that much like me, Rocky is often written off. He is labelled as the wrong shape, as too old or as having terrible technique. I smile to myself sometimes as people talk to me about how I run and how big I am. "You're too big to run distance," they say. "You haven't spent enough time on the bike to be able to do 150 miles a day!" Pain is pain; it's there whether you are fat or thin, black or white, short or tall. How you deal with the pain and the hard work is what sets you apart.

The people that say I am the wrong shape are right, but I can still move. The people that say my technique is poor are correct, but I can still get there. The people that say I don't spend enough time cycling to do 150 miles are right, but I still got it done. The difference?

Desire?

Pride?

Motivation?

Help for Heroes?

.............maybe all of these in some way but for me the answer is simple. The answer is Rocky. Never ever give up. If you lose, you learn. If you win, remember how.

I was on the bike for the second time in quick succession, after finishing on the bike the previous day. The roads so far had actually been quite pleasant with only a few potholes and with long stretches where I could open my legs and power on. We left Philadelphia as quickly as we had arrived. The site seeing was over and we were back on the road. Until this point we had been using relatively quiet roads, leafy suburbs and long straight streets. As we powered towards Washington the maps said that the most direct route was down the interstate. We didn't think anything of this and simply joined the traffic on the interstate. I was sat up front with the RV tucked in behind me to block the traffic. I sat at a steady 27mph and ploughed through the miles towards the capital. It was still early in the day; we had come through Philadelphia first thing, after finishing the previous day right on the outskirts of the city. It was a decent press to get to the capital but we would camp just outside the city that evening.

Day 2 was another long day. Heading down a large descent with traffic building into three lanes my tyre blew out. My back end snaking all the way to the foot of the hill. Any blow out is scary; a blow out at 40mph on a push bike makes your bottom twitch for a few days after, I can tell you! It was late in the day when the tyre burst, I was tired and the team had been navigating me through the streets of Philadelphia (brilliant Bruce Springsteen song) all morning and then on busy roads in the afternoon. We were all working hard just to keep me moving and alive. With the tyre fixed and the evening drawing in, I needed one last push. The traffic moving towards Washington was thick and full of people who did not want a Lycra clad Englishman holding up their commute. I couldn't relax at all, maintaining a constant pace was difficult. I had been on the bike all day after leaving Philadelphia, and everyone around me had been at work. Everyone wanted to get settled down for the evening, me more so than anyone.

Our first brush with the law came on the second day. I had loved cycling down the interstates, the climbing was relatively easy, the roads were wide and everything seemed to be going well, then on the radio I was told to stop. As I turned back to check the RV and the rest of the team I noticed the Blue flashing light behind the RV, "Crap," I thought, "what have we done to deserve being pulled over?" I walked my bike back to the RV where the Policeman was debriefing the team on why we were not allowed to ride a push bike down the interstate. "You can't ride down the interstate man, you'll get yourself killed!" At first, I thought, well, I have been doing it for the last 6 hours and I am still here but then I realised exactly what we were doing. We were on the major commuter road, heading into the capital city of America at rush hour. For context in the UK, imagine the M25 at rush hour, and then imagine my pasty little body weaving along on a bike. The boys in Blue had a point and with that I jumped in the RV and headed for some quieter roads.

The evening was spent in one of the more amusing RV sites we would come across. We arrived into the site in complete darkness, large bugs splattered across our windscreen, we were tired and in need of a shower. We completed the 464,746 point turn to get the RV into the right bay and opened the door, huge mistake. As the door opened the light from the RV shone across the jungle we now realised we had parked in. The entire cast of 'A Bug's Life' flew into the RV, I think there may have been some animals that appeared in 'Jurassic Park' now flying round the RV, as well. It was at this moment that I realised that none of us were Bear Grylls, in fact you would have thought none of us had ever been outside before. The screams echoed around the RV site like something out of a horror film, "Get it....squish it....kill it!" the screeches said. Bearing in mind that I had just completed 150 miles on a bike, I was not leaping about to kill the winged crocodile that was flying round the RV, but luckily (unlucky for the insect) it did come near me. The bug was no more. The team appeared from under the bed covers and behind the curtains where they had been hiding. The noises of the animals continued long into the night, sleep was at a premium.

Chapter 7

I thought it would be bigger?

Not sleeping and the RV were two things linked very closely, add into the mix being parked in the middle of a great big forest with 20,000 bugs that could, if they wanted to, kill you - sleep didn't happen. The problem with no sleep is not just the fact you are shattered but that your body has no time to recover. Running and cycling every day is horrible enough, now I was sleep deprived and in desperate need of recovery. I felt like things were starting to stack up against me.

Washington was not what I expected at all, but I am not sure what I actually expected. Did I expect to see the President out walking his dog at the White House or did I think it might be a little bit more like London as this was the capital after all? What we got was a very cosmopolitan area with a very angry under belly. Signs of protest covered most railings, protesting it seemed about whatever they could. The inevitable Trump protests adorned the majority of the posters we saw. We tried hard to avoid any talk of politics. A simple reason for this, I had absolutely no idea which area supported which part of the government. There was as much for Trump as there was against it. Seemed to me like democracy at its finest?

Like with many places we stayed and visited, I wished we had had a little more time to look around. The bits of Washington I saw I didn't enjoy. It came across as very corporate with people in suits carrying overpriced coffees scurrying along the pavement, ears permanently glued to their phones. The world could have been ending but it seemed that everyone in Washington would have had something better to do than save it.

The obligatory sightseeing took place. I love to take in the sights of any place I visit, see what all the fuss is about and learn about the history and culture of that place. Washington has some history, The White House for one is a place steeped in American History. As we stood with about 1,000 Japanese tourists I couldn't help but think, "Isn't it bigger?" The film Independence Day depicts the White House blowing up in quite impressive style. The truth is, I can't imagine the explosion would be that big. As magnificent as the White House is, it's just a pretty big house. If we are playing Top Trumps, Buckingham Palace wins hands down, every time. We stood for about ten minutes, jostling with the other tourists for the best place to take the picture. "Well, that's that done," we thought as we trundled off back to the RV.

As we got towards the end of a section of greenery we saw some more touristy-type people heading down a private road, let's follow them we thought as we still had about 10 minutes until we needed to be back at the RV. As we did we saw a larger crowd than the 1,000 Japanese people we had just encountered. It didn't take us long to realise that we had been taking photos of the back of the White House! It did look a touch more impressive from the front, although, it was still just a pretty big house.

Day 3 was all about running. It was the first time I had put my trainers on since New York. New York had soaked me to the core, my trainers had felt heavy during the running as the water had saturated them. Washington was different. The rain from New York was nowhere to be seen, instead we had blazing hot sun. Sun cream was applied in force; I looked like I had been painted with emulsion as I plodded along the pavement but I had a smile on my face because the sun was shining!

For the team on the RV a running day was much better for them. It was boring if they had to stay on the RV as they did when I was on the bike, but they could at least get off and run with me when I was running. My feet had taken a real battering when they were wet in New York and my toe nails were already becoming soft. I knew right then that it wouldn't be long before a decision needed to be made about whether I would let my toe nails fall out naturally or whether I would have to pull them out with pliers. On the original Epic Run the pliers had been needed, the nails had needed a little extra coaxing out of the nice, warm nail bed they were in.

After the previous day's run in with the law, we stayed solely to surface streets and highways but even the highways were a little too congested at times. As we moved away from the capital the traffic calmed and the landscape became greener, trees now lined the road sides and fields spread out as far as the eye could see. It was good running for the rest of the day. Sun shining, light breeze at my back – the conditions were as near to perfect as they could be.

Towards the end of the day I was running along the side of the road, it was very much how I had imagined America would be. Little towns with local grocery stores, porch swings and picket fences. In each garden the American flag was flying proudly. I was running in a little haze when...BANG! A car had gotten a little too close to me and caught my elbow jolting me out of my near sedated running state. As with anything it was the shock that frightened me, the car didn't do any major damage just a little knock, but for the rest of the day all I could think was, "A little knock when I'm running isn't too bad. I'm only doing 6mph. A little knock when I'm on my bike, though, and I'm in some serious trouble!"

Chapter 8

Like pedalling in a Greenhouse with the heating on

Day 4 and I'm back on the bike....well...not quite. While moving the bike in the morning at the RV site, we managed to break the seat stem, meaning that the seat would not stay at the right height for me whilst I was cycling. Day 4 saw us travelling from Hagerstown to Washington, this time it was not Washington DC but a much smaller town.

I wasn't able to use the bike first thing in the morning which meant getting changed and running again, not a prospect, I relished but a necessity if we were to keep moving. I ran through small towns and villages along quiet country roads. In my headphones the words of Bruce Springsteen describing the towns of America were starting to make more and more sense. Some of the towns we passed were desolate lonely places - places reminiscent of those from zombie apocalypse-type films. There is nothing open at 6am and so the chances of getting the bike fixed early are evidently slim. We crawl along at a snail's pace, my legs screaming at me, they feel like they are being tenderised with each step I take.

The shake of my quad muscles across my thigh pulls tiny ligaments and sends a shooting pain both up and down my legs. I think back to Scotland, to the Lochs and to the pain. "You got through that," I tell myself, "you got through." I repeat this over and over in my head.

We arrived in a small town, the name of it even now escapes me, and pain flooded my mind. It was still only 8am in the morning; the majority of the town was asleep. As I crept slowly along the streets we saw the light of a car garage on, just off the street. We all agreed that it was worth a try. The garage looked pretty much how you would imagine an old American car mechanic's garage to look. Beat up old vehicles were dotted around the place and parts of old pickup trucks were hanging from the walls. The large Ford sign sat crooked on top of the roof, a long time since it had been cleaned or painted.

The part that was missing from my bike was the collar off the seat post, the little part that makes the seat post grip and not drop through. Such an unbelievably simple piece of equipment but one that we did not have a spare for and the garage clearly didn't have one lying around either.

I decided to carry on running not wanting to stop as I was already massively behind for the day. The team stayed at the garage with my bike, scratching around for something to try and hold my saddle in place.

They caught me up only a mile down the road; I had pushed on and out of the other side of the town and was headed into wide open country. The Bruce Springsteen song Darlington County bounced around my brain for some reason. I have no idea where Darlington County is and I am sure I was miles away from it, but right at that point the words seemed quite apt. The kind old man at the garage had managed to shackle together something that would hold my seat stem in place, I'm sure he may never know that that exact seat stem stayed entirely the same for the next 2,500 miles whilst travelling over some of the harshest roads a bike could ever cover – perhaps one day he will read these words and if you are reading this Sir, I would like to say to you a huge 'THANK YOU!'. The bike was now sorted and humanity had shown its beautiful true colours once again.

When I ran I maintained about a 6mph average, which meant I was running 10 minute miles, but on the bike I could eat up the miles, covering 25 miles an hour. It meant that I felt like I had moved.

When I ran sometimes it felt like I hadn't moved very far; the landscape, the signposts, the people - they all stayed the same, whereas on the bike you could make real headway and move over state lines much quicker.

The climbing on Day 4 will be something I will never forget. I think it's probably more the accomplishment that I won't forget, the sheer brutality of the heat and humidity coupled with the ferocity of the climbs made me feel even more triumphant. There didn't seem to be anything flat any more, New York's streets were a distant memory and the climbs just kept on coming. As we pushed further into Pennsylvania the humidity seemed to get worse, as I pushed into my pedals the sweat that had accumulated in my shoes was forced out of the front like wringing out a sponge. Breathing in the warm moist air was like cycling in a greenhouse. The sun seemed to be focussed on only me, it felt almost like I had my own personal spotlight.

I asked the team to drive on ahead, I was at my slowest, the traffic was building up behind the RV and I knew the mountains were going to be a battle. The steepest climb on Day 4 was a 2,915ft climb - that isn't really too bad but when this was the steepest climb of 7 that I did that day, it just seems like the odds are stacking against you. The blow out from earlier in the trip meant that the descents were done with a little more caution by this point. I braced, the weight pushed back over my rear tyre, I was trying my hardest to maintain a high speed and get down the mountains in one piece. Each climb I conquered the team were at the top cheering and whooping, doing everything they could to keep my spirits up. I loved them for that.

The top of every mountain has a sign saying 'Welcome to the Top', or 'Well done'. It has a message that lets you know that you have achieved something to get there that day. I loved these little bits at the top. The problem was that at the bottom of each mountain there was a sign saying the exact opposite - "YOU ARE AT THE FOOT OF MOUNT......." These messages really push you close to breaking point, they allow you to know what is coming and that is a real challenge.

At the end of the day, a couple of brilliant things happened. One was some support from a person who had seen me on the bike, she wrote:

Kelsey Shantz @kelseysh... · 27/07/2017 ⌄
Just passed charity cyclist/runner
@sam_boatwright1 near Everett, PA. This stretch of PA is long even by car. Good luck!

♡   ↺5   ♥ 4   ✉

It gives you a massive boost when local people know how hard the road is as well, and if it wasn't apparent enough I think they could see the suffering on my face. I suppose if it was easy then everyone would be doing it. I didn't see one other cyclist that day.

The second brilliant thing needs a bit of an introduction. The previous day in the RV site I had taken an ice bath in our inflatable paddling pool. As I have explained to many people, we were not a team of doctors and medics, we were a bunch of friends and colleagues who wanted to have an adventure. The inflatable paddling pool was a life saver and a thoroughly brilliant idea. There are few steps required in making the best ice baths.

1. Fill paddling pool with cold water so it's deeper than your legs when you sit down.
2. Chuck a few bags of ice in.
3. Sit down and swear a lot.
4. Get out and apologise to the families in the RV around yours

The end of Day 4 didn't end with an ice bath in a paddling pool; instead we ended up in the river. What better way to cool yourself down before calling it a night than jumping in a river? I say jump, it was more of a geriatric lying down, but it was still amazing. The team stood at the side and laughed as I shrieked at the freezing temperature of the water.

As much as I loathe them, the ice baths are an essential part of any endurance event. They become a daily ritual, and they become a necessity. However, at the end of this day, a dip in an icy river was a wonderful and welcome alternative.

Chapter 9

The Kindness of Strangers

Matty and Hannan, thank you.

Humidity was something I started to get used to. I don't mean get used to as in liked or enjoyed, but more so accepted as a constant, something that was always just there. There is not much in the UK that can help you train for humidity, no areas that even come close, especially not in Yorkshire. The nearest thing we get is when we boil the kettle in a small room, or the air conditioning breaks at the gym, even then you can crack a window and let some air in. The problem in Pennsylvania, was that there was no window to open or fan to put on. It was constant body-sapping humidity from the moment I set out in the morning till the moment I set foot back on the RV at night.

As I pressed up towards Pittsburgh, it was the first time that some of the team would be leaving us. We arrived as a team of 6, but for the next 2 weeks it would be down to a team of 4. We were 50 miles outside of Pittsburgh and the 2 team members needed dropping off at Pittsburgh train station. It was a running day and so I set off running with Kerry (my now wife and team member) and the rest of the team headed to Pittsburgh to drop the guys off.

The morning was deadly calm, the early mist settled on the hills around us, steam rose from the tarmac and the heat of the day began to build. We plodded out of the RV site and onto a highway, it was an old country road and, at 6am, it was quiet. The odd car rolled passed but there was no actual traffic.

Kerry and I chatted as we ran. The road undulated like a camel's back for miles upon miles. Some of the climbs forced our pace to slow down but we remained happily trotting away soaking up the scenery, all the while edging slowly closer to Pittsburgh.

Sweat leaked out of me all morning, that's the problem with humidity, it's not like the blazing sun, the heat is different, and the way you sweat is different. The humidity made my clothes feel like they were sticking to me, like my own clothes were suffocating me. At each rest point, I could feel the weight of my clothes pulling down against my body. It was energy sapping work. With the RV in Pittsburgh, there was no support vehicle. Much like on the original 'Epic Run' as soon as the support vehicle wasn't there you would become a "normal" person. To any passers-by, you are just two people out for a morning run, you are not two people on an 'Epic Adventure' anymore. The RV also offers sanctuary when things get too much or you need to take 5 minutes.

Within the first hour we had drunk all of our water. We had estimated that the journey into Pittsburgh and back should take them approximately one and a half to a maximum of two hours. We had run for two hours and we had just hit a clearing that joined onto a very busy highway, a dual lane highway with fast traffic heading in both directions. Trucks rumbled past at alarming speeds, every now and again there was a massive vibrating shudder as they strayed onto the rumble strips at the side of the road, this did not fill me with much confidence.

There was a small shop across the road and luckily I had stuffed $20 into my sock just in case of such an emergency. The shop looked like it might have some kind of liquid refreshment. We sat outside the little shop with our refreshments, sweat dripping off of us and making puddles on the floor.

Over two hours had now passed since the guys had set off for Pittsburgh so we knew they couldn't be too much longer. A quick message was sent to see what time they would be with us. The reply was not what we wanted. The team were not even at the train station when they text us, meaning it was going to be more than 2 hours until they caught up with us. Kerry had already run 12 miles (13.5 being her furthest ever to date). We had to keep moving, the longer we stayed sat doing nothing the longer my day would be. With the remainder of the emergency $20 quickly spent on Gatorade and water we set off down the busy highway towards Pittsburgh, once again.

Running on a pavement is different to running on the road. If you have never done any road running you would think this was stupid. A pavement, in general, is very smooth tarmac; your trainers can roll across the top of it with little friction. The camber of a pavement is also different, it helps the water drain off the pavement but it isn't a steep camber that your legs feel, much more gentle and forgiving. A road tends to have larger chunks of stone in the tarmac, meaning that it's not quite as smooth. The friction created against the road therefore is much more significant. Over a few strides this is minimal, over 50 miles' worth of strides this becomes much harder work. The road down this particular highway had large chunks, added into the mix with the humidity and the passing traffic, the running was tough, very tough.

Drained, sweaty and already tired we bumbled down the road side, sometimes jumping onto the grass verge to avoid the oncoming trucks. For those in the UK, we were running on the left hand side of the road with the traffic coming at us, at this particular time that was our only option, as the other side of the road didn't even have a white line to run inside of. The dust and dirt erupted into a mini tornado every time another truck stormed past, taking visibility to near zero and adding another layer of grime to your skin.

We hit 20 miles of running and we were losing patience, it's strange what happens as you get more and more tired. Decision making becomes difficult, simple things you would normally take for granted become hard to process, should I or shouldn't I cross the road becomes a potentially life altering decision. We knew that we needed to stop, we knew we couldn't keep going for much longer on that road without support.

As we crept down the roadside, the curb stepped back and buildings lined the road side. We needed water again – badly – and we had used up all of our emergency funding. About 300 metres up the road we saw the start of a sign saying 'Gym.........' The rest of the sign was cut off by another building. As we chatted we decided that the gym would definitely have water in it, we would simply explain to them what we were doing and we were sure they would let us in, after all America loves its veterans and we were doing it for them. As we approached the building we noticed that it was not a gym like we had thought but, in fact, a gymnasium where dancers go to practise. We felt there was still hope of getting some water, though.

One thing that the British are very aware of when in America is the fact that every man and his dog, and the dog's cousin for that matter have a gun, and they know how to use it. There was no one in the building at all, we popped our head around the corner and in the best Queen's English shouted "Hello, anyone here?" No reply. As we moved away from the building a pickup truck turned onto the car park. "Can I help you?" the man asked in an accent a little different from that in Washington. The accent was a little bit more country than we had heard previously. We explained who we were where we going and why we were in America. A huge smile appeared across the stranger's face, he darted inside and quickly reappeared, arms fully loaded with Gatorade and water, enough to satiate the thirst of thousands never mind a dehydrated and dusty couple from Yorkshire.

After posing for a few pictures and posting on a few social networks about the stranger's business, we said our 'thank-yous' and began thinking about the next few miles ahead of us. As we turned to run again the RV came over the crest of the hill. I could have cried. My legs were empty, Kerry was shattered and I needed the protection of the RV on this road.

Along with the return of the RV, we had been given another very welcome boost. We now knew that that evening we would be able to have a warm shower, a home cooked meal and some new company. Through the power of social media, we were going to be taken care of by a wonderful couple in Pittsburgh. It was a welcome change from the tiny cubicle shower of the RV and that night we well and truly feasted - it was brilliant!

We slept on the RV that night just down the road from where we had been shown the incredible hospitality. As we bunked down for the evening our mobile phones went crazy, all buzzing and beeping simultaneously, the RV must have nearly moved with the vibration.

TEXT ALERT: WEATHER WARNING FLASH FLOOD ALERT FOR PITTSBURGH AREA

Almost instantly as the message came through it started raining. When I'm at home in bed, I love the sound of rain hitting the window, its gives you that feeling of warmth and security. This was not the same; it could not have been more different. The rain drops felt like bowling balls hitting the RV, lightning crashed all around us, and the thunder bellowed in the heavens so loud and angry that the RV seemed to cower in fear. The humidity of the day was being broken in the most tremendous way. I lay there thinking to myself, "Are we even going to be here in the morning?"

Chapter 10

Can You Tell Me the Way to Columbia?

Everything hurt - everything. Not just my legs or my feet, but everything. I felt like I had been giving a piggy back to the heaviest person on the planet. I wittered to myself all morning on the bike, cursing the stupid idea of ever coming to America in the first place. "What sort of an idiot does this for their summer holidays?" I asked myself. "What sort of an imbecile is out in the pouring rain on a bike that changes gears whenever it feels like it?" I barked.

I kept myself busy most of the morning cursing the film Forest Gump. "It can't have been real," I said to myself, "it is utter rubbish! There is no way he ran all that way and didn't swear once!" I was swearing at anything and everything, if a squirrel farted 3 miles away it got a piece of my mind, but mainly, I was swearing at myself.

I also couldn't help but swear at the rain, it was becoming a joke now. The maps we were following were pretty much of no use now as the roads were being closed due to flooding. Imagine if you can, been in a foreign country, then imagine you have decided (stupidly decided - I might add) to run and cycle across it (around 3000 miles). Imagine then that you don't have a clue where you're going and to top it all off after 6 days of running and cycling you end up getting lost and it becomes apparent that you have simply travelled in a big circle – I do not have to imagine this, I have done it! As you can probably appreciate, when I began to see the same shops coming back into sight my heart sank. I couldn't get mad at the team; they were doing everything they could to make sure I was safe and to help me get to the other side of America. It is at times like this, the times where you want to cry, that you realise that you have just hit bottom.

My ass was sore from the saddle, my legs were empty, water dripped off of the end of my nose, a constant torturous drip, the kind you start to focus on and then get angry at. Just as this entire morning was seemingly building to a scream-infested, crying-fit of a climax, Helen wound down the window and asked me:

"So, how far is it to Colombia?"

"Well Helen, it's about 5000 miles I reckon and it's on a different continent! I don't think I will make it today!" I replied forcing the words out through tears of laughter.

"OOOOOO...that's a long way!" was the only reply Helen could muster.

This is the reason that I had the team there, something so simple put a big smile back on my face.

It was now 1 o'clock in the afternoon and I had spent the entire morning cycling in a deluge of rain that had continued from the previous evening. Saturated and thoroughly fed up I pushed onwards towards Columbus.

We were heading out of the sticky and sweaty state of Pennsylvania and on in to Ohio.

Prior to my departure I had been sent some kit to use whilst I was in America, the majority of it was clothing to keep me warm which I didn't think I would ever need but I was happy to take any donations. During a torrential downpour I wore every piece of clothing that they had sent me. It was scuba diving clothing and it proved brilliant on the bike, especially when it was raining.

We had come out of the south side of Pittsburgh, heading west towards Columbus. Earlier after we had been told we were not allowed to cycle on the interstates, we had tried to mirror the line of the interstate as much as possible, where quite often the older, quieter highways ran parallel.

As we moved into Ohio the weather changed again, the sun came out and the rain disappeared, clothing was quickly shed and the horrific morning of rain was forgotten in a haze of blistering heat. The little towns look so much more appealing in the sun, the white picket fences reflect the sunlight and help to brighten up the day. Moving through the little towns, families sat on their porches, sometimes sitting on a little swing seat and children played with baseballs and basketballs in the streets - this was Middle America, deep in the heart of the country. I loved it.

I was in the saddle eleven and a half hours – however, taking into account the breaks and rest stops, it totalled thirteen hours. From the rain soaked morning in Pittsburgh we had arrived just outside Columbus. It was late in the evening and navigation was the last thing on our minds, we avoided the city centre and set up camp on the outskirts of the city.

Chapter 11

Ohio

I have never been one for big cities or large tourist destinations. When I arrive somewhere I put my running shoes on and go out and explore. What better way to see a place than to get lost in it? I can safely say we got lost in America - a lot. Ohio was a beautiful place to run, a balmy twenty eight degrees with quaint towns every few miles and rolling fields as far as the eye can see. Like everything in America, the fields are not higgledy-piggledy like in the UK, they are clean straight lines, uniform and organised. I guess with so much space there is not the demand for land like there is in Britain. The streets are in blocks, the crops are regimented - they have never even considered a dilapidated dry stone wall dissecting a field at a 34 degree angle.

Ohio was so much more pleasant than Pennsylvania, the muggy heat had disappeared, and it was drier now. Early morning was brilliant, the stillness and serenity of a country morning, I had not experienced anything like this since I ran in Scotland on the first 'Epic Run' and prior to that I can only recall such peacefulness as a child in Malham. The tranquillity and the weather had meant that I had run a 4 hour and 17 minute marathon on the first morning in Ohio.

Columbus, Ohio was one of my favourite cities. Cities are not usually my favourite places, but Columbus is different. Columbus has a small town feel but with large city buildings. We moved along through the city, prior to the commuter infiltration. The architecture of the city is beautiful, nothing garish or lavish, just simplicity and class. Its buildings like its inhabitants are friendly and thoughtful. The buildings feel to be part of the landscape, like they have always been there, as if they are natural.

Out of the city, we were into the countryside again. The seamless, effortless transition into nature wondrous in its elegance. As we left Columbus, cornfields filled my view on one side with soya beans on the other. The corn stood tall, ripe and ready in many instances. The fields went for miles into the distance. I couldn't help but think of the amount of corn and soya bean produced in this area, it must surely cover the entire world's need for these vegetables. There is acre upon acre of plantation, a massive contrast to the concrete jungle of New York, we had left behind a week earlier.

Running along to side of the road cloaked by cornfields you notice how well kept the small pieces of grass are that border the fields. One of the highest selling items in Ohio must be the 'sit on lawnmower', never in my life have I seen so many people mowing their grass. I watched as an elderly gentleman manoeuvred his mower up and down the roadside, cutting his small strip of grass that bordered the enormous corn field. It seemed quite pointless to me, to be cutting the grass when only a few inches from the grass was 6ft high corn, but it gave the old fella something to do!

As I approached another farm I noticed that the RV had stopped and was speaking to the farmer. He was not mowing the grass but had come out on his 'sit on lawnmower' to see what it was we were doing. His name was Burt Montgomery, a 90 year old Korea Veteran who had farmed this land since he was 7 years old, his sons and now grandsons still farmed this 2,000 acre farm. He recanted tales of his youth and how the farm had developed over the years. We told him what I was doing and who I was raising money for. As we told him about 'Help for Heroes' he paused, took out his wallet (which by the looks of it was as old as he was) and gave us $20 for our charity. A veteran helping other veterans! Burt, by the way, didn't look a day over 50 - maybe the farming life is what has kept him looking so young. Also, his little strip of grass was immaculate! Burt Montgomery another true hero in a world which is apparently lacking them.

After a week on the road we were ready for a bed, to get off the RV and get a change of scenery for the evening, cabin fever was beginning to take hold. A friend from my university days had moved out to America a few years earlier, originally relocating to LA they had now settled in a small leafy town called Loveland, Ohio. A better name for a town, I think you would struggle to find. We dined that evening with family and friends, a beautiful home in the heart of Ohio. We told stories of the road and our adventures so far. I sat with Sion and laughed about our university days, remarking on how incredible it was that we were both sat in Ohio 15 years later. The kids playing and running around took my mind away from what was still to come. You can always count on kids to raise your spirits, they don't understand failure, they have no concept of time and space, for them we were on a "Big Barbie Truck" and I was just riding my little bike. The fact that we had been going for a week and still had 2,000 miles to go through deserts and over mountain ranges was not something that they had even considered. Thank you for your smiles Griffydd and Bronwen, one day I hope you will realise how much you and your family helped me.

Goodbyes are always hard, even more so when a 3 year old wants to come with you. After the goodbyes were finished I pressed out of Loveland on my bike. Our final destination for this day was a place called Batesville, how very American I thought. Batesville, however, was fairly uninspiring, just another town, but for us a stop off on the way to bigger things.

After Batesville, we headed into Indiana and up towards Chicago. The heat changed all the time, sometimes muggy and humid other times dry and baking hot. The RV was used more as a cooling station; cold showers becoming a frequent occurrence during my day. They helped immensely in settling down my heart rate and just calming my body temperature to somewhere near normality. During the planning, the heat of the country was always on my mind, I tried my hardest to block it out but it was becoming more of a battle against the heat than against the road.

Hitting double digits on the days done was a massive boost. 10 days and we were still in the game. Cycling in Indiana is hard, not hard like mountains and deserts, it's more the monotony of the landscape. Straight roads and cornfields, they are endless and after a couple of days of them, they are mind-numbingly boring. The roads are so straight and the heat so intense that as you look into the distance the road hazes into the heat and it becomes a blurred wave of colour, mentally having apparently no goal to aim for is hard work. On Day 10, we stopped and rested in a small town called Frankfurt, like the previous towns across the country the water tower stood prominent on the edge of the town with Frankfurt written on it in large black letters. You can see the water towers before you see the towns, a clear indication that you are nearing civilisation once again.

We closed in on Chicago, once again the fields gave way to the streets and the traffic built to a point where I couldn't safely run or cycle on the road. On the outskirts of Chicago, I jumped in the RV and we headed to a hotel. We had decided to stay in a hotel that evening, we hoped to have a decent night's sleep before the real Route 66 began.

Completing day 10 I was shattered, I needed sleep and I needed to stop. I lay in the back of the RV, a window above my head and I watched for a few minutes as the world whizzed by, my eyes became heavy and within seconds I was gone. Completely exhausted, I drifted into a deep slumber.

Chapter 12

The Start of Route 66

What an anti-climax, I had built this up in my head as some sort of magical occasion, the pot of gold, a major milestone of the trip. Instead it was some decrepit sign, covered in gum and stickers down a random street in the middle of Chicago. For something as iconic as Route 66, they could have done so much more, in all honesty you would have no idea you were on Route 66 until about 200 miles out of Chicago. Kerry once again joined me at the start of the run, the RV again struggling to support us due to the busy streets and tight turns. We agreed to meet up on the outskirts of the city, about 10 miles from where we were. It was a pleasant morning in Chicago with a morning mist sitting over the city keeping a little warmth inside it.

Navigating out of the city was not too bad at all, we knew once we got onto one street we could follow that all the way out and that we would eventually meet up with the highway we needed to take us down to Gardener, the next town on our list. We passed through the different neighbourhoods of Chicago, the smells and sites of this vibrant city hitting you as you passed along their streets. Chicago offers you something different from other large cities; it has a small urban feel to it rather than big city life. Sitting on the banks of the great lake it moulds itself neatly around it as if connected by some cosmic bond. The people of Chicago are friendly and helpful; nothing is too much trouble for them. It is nicknamed the Windy City and thankfully the wind wasn't against us during our visit.

The 12 days we had done had taken their toll on my body. I was a stone down in weight. One stone in 12 days, beats most of the fad diets we see so much on TV and a perfect way to teach people some very basic rules about weight loss. Firstly, if you burn more than you consume you will lose weight. For example, I was burning on average 12,000 calories a day, but as much as I wanted to eat I couldn't physically consume 12,000 calories worth of food, the end result is weight loss. This would be the same result no matter what the numbers were as long as the calories consumed are less than the calories burnt weight will be lost - but I do admit that this is quite an extreme fitness regime!

As much as I was burning, I also had to take into account that I had to keep my engine going, as well. This is what most people cannot comprehend, starvation is not the way to lose weight, quite the opposite in fact and this seems to most people contradictory. I needed to make sure my body had something to burn, it needed good fuel to get through. An analogy I often use is that of a car or a train - the engine needs fuel to run, too little and you will breakdown, too much and you will flood and also inevitably breakdown. Take on what you need, when you need it.

My diet and eating by this point was honed to perfection, but like many things the perfection had been achieved through trial and error, and there had been a number of errors. This type of task was not something any of us had ever done before and we had no one else to follow as there is no one else that has ever done this before either. My daily intake looked something close to this:

- Breakfast – This varied between eggs, cereal and fresh fruit salad.
- Mid-Morning - Fruit salad with yogurt and granola
- Dinner* – 6 scrambled eggs and more fruit salad
- Mid Afternoon – Protein bar
- Tea* – This varied between Tuna Pasta Bake, Spaghetti Bolognese, Chilli, Pizza and BBQ.

(*For people not from Yorkshire, dinner is lunch and tea is dinner)

It was nothing too fancy, it was nothing out of the ordinary. The team looked after me; this was my fuel every day, it worked. I think some people see something like this challenge and they believe you have to have some special diet or you have to be some sort of freak. Keeping fit and eating well is like anything, it's all about balance.

Chicago was gone, quickly left behind like so many of the cities and towns before it, but it would be forever remembered as the start of Route 66. Out of the city, we were onto quieter roads again, the interstate, though, was never far away, the rumble of the traffic a constant reminder.

Most of you will be forgiven for thinking that Route 66 is one road from Chicago to LA and that navigation should be easy. We thought that, too - how wrong we were. The Old Route 66 is a series of old roads and highways weaving their way through small towns and clusters of houses, the road itself breaking and buckling with the lack of maintenance. Alongside this is the interstate, a giant beast of a road that cuts straight through the land. The old road bobs and weaves with the undulating land, dipping and diving with the landscape, the interstate pays no attention to what is around it and bulldozes nose first straight through, unforgiving and brutal.

We followed the old road where we could, so that we could visit the smaller towns and villages that lay along the road. We saw the old gas stations, some abandoned years ago, others faintly clinging to that little piece of the American dream. They have kept their old fashioned pumps and iconic signs, hoping (in vein, I believe) to draw the tourists from the much busier interstate. Abandoned businesses and houses would become a common site as we pushed across the country, some still inhabited but in dire need of restoration. It is not until you are there, stood within it, that you see how much the interstate has taken from these people. The Old Route 66 may be challenging but it is worth the hardship to help support these people.

I ran from sunrise to sunset, eventually coming to an end on a long straight road with the train track running parallel. The train-lines are different in America. I am sure in the cities they are much like the train-lines in Britain, busy and full of commuters, but head to the mid-west and what you find is not commuter trains but large haulage trains with carriages numbering in the hundreds. A train would pass and it would still be passing 10 minutes later, the banging of the carriages would be almost deafening.

Chapter 13

The Magic Sponge

The alternative title to this chapter would have been "head wind" or to be less polite "a b@st*rd of a head-wind". As mentioned previously, America has some very, very straight roads, which for somethings are brilliant, for example, if the wind is behind you. Unfortunately, when the wind is right at you it is soul destroying. The part I struggled with most was knowing that the wind that was coming from the West and going to the East and that it was now going to be there for the remainder of the journey. It took me back to Scotland and the start line at John 0'Groats, no matter how hard I pushed, I felt like I was going backwards. If I stood and tried to pedal out of my saddle I made myself bigger and the wind caught me and pushed me back further. Tears streamed down my face, the wind ferocious in its efforts to break me.

We were heading to a Town called Springfield, it is the home of Abraham Lincoln and of course The Simpsons. Sadly, that is about as much trivia as I can give you about Springfield as the main thoughts going through my mind were how to stop my bum from hurting. I was wearing full tights and a long-sleeved top;

the temperature had dropped considerably. The bike was starting to hurt me worse than I thought it would have. At home, I spend every day on some sort of bike, whether it's a spin bike, watt bike or my own push bike so I thought that the saddle soreness would not be a problem - how wrong I was. I longed for smooth tarmac but in order to avoid pain this nearly had to be as smooth as a bowling alley. Every slight bobble in the road was met with immense pain. I was shuffling and shimmying in the saddle trying to get just a second's respite from the horrors of it. There was no escaping it, it got to a point where I could manage about 2 minutes in the saddle and then I had to stand up and get out of the saddle all the while knowing at some point I would have to sit down again. I had taken every piece of advice thrown at me - wear pants, don't wear pants, get well-padded shorts, wear a thin pad and many others. These are all excellent ideas but unfortunately none of them helped. I was applying chamois cream by the handful, not a pleasant site for anyone. If you don't know what this cream is, it is cream you apply to your posterior to stop the chafing. It looks and feels quite strange. I was at a point of desperation, a point where I was breaking the day into tiny 20-minute blocks and then getting off the bike and walking around to try and ease the pain, even if only for a few minutes. At the back of your mind, every stop you take you know is a little bit more added on to the end of your day because whichever way you look at it you have to get the mileage done.

We pulled over in a small town called Lincoln. Whilst I walked around very slowly allowing the blood to flow back into my butt cheeks, the team went and bought a sponge. It wasn't anything special or fancy, a

$4 sponge from a random grocery shop. You will not see sponges become an essential part of a cyclist kit bag but to me and the team this sponge was magical. I stuffed the sponge down the back of my shorts and sat on the bike, in comparison to earlier I could have been sat on a deck chair at the beach or even better on the sofa in my living room. The pain and torture from the morning had gone. I gave an orgasmic sigh as I sat on the saddle, the relief, I am sure, was evident all over my face.

The head wind was still proving to be a problem, however. I was not able to hit my averages and so my mileage was down on the day. Normally I can average between 27-30 miles per hour, I was only pushing at around 22 miles per hour. It was painful, gruelling work. The sponge was doing its job in protecting my rear but I was emptying my energy reserves quickly, expending vast amounts of energy just to maintain the current average speed.

My headphones beat music out, large anthemic tunes from Bruce (The Boss) Springsteen played and I sang at the top of my lungs as I weaved my way along the highway. When it wasn't 'The Boss' I turned a little heavier and went for Linkin Park's Hybrid Theory, a classic in my opinion. There was the odd occasion where I wanted something a little lighter in order to try and bring a little happiness into the world. I am a big believer in trying to change people's perceptions of how they see the world. I am 6 foot 3 inches tall, I am heavily tattooed and probably to most I look quite intimidating. So, while I was cycling through deepest Illinois I decided to camp things up a little bit by singing some show tunes, I particularly enjoyed Joseph and the Amazing Technicoloured Dreamcoat. It is always good to see a person's face when you change their opinion of you, especially when it is for the better!

I was definitely finding running days much easier than on the bike. Whether this is because I felt more confident running or because I knew people could be out running with me, I don't know. The running days were taking me on average about 11 or 12 hours to complete, they were long days, but the bike days were even longer taking me about 12 to 15 hours. Each time I knew the bike was coming up, I would be dreading it. When I was running I was already thinking about the bike the next day, and how much it would hurt. I would be looking at the tarmac and the landscape and thinking to myself how much it was going to hurt. Every so often I would descend a hill and think that this might be ok on a bike. However, at that point I would turn the corner and the climb would be brutal, the tarmac would be all broken and disjointed and I would be thankful that I was running.

Day 13 - I was off the bike and running strong, the magic sponge was rested for the day and I was able to plod along. I had started to break my days down into more manageable blocks, this gave me something to work towards but it also allowed the team the chance to come out and run in different stages. I didn't want one of them getting hurt and not being able to run with me anymore. All of them played their part, sometimes it might have been a short two mile stretch but every time that they ran with me helped me immeasurably.

I had broken the 1000-mile mark, a sign on the side of the road told me it was 1907 miles to LA. I remember a friend telling me about when they ran their first marathon, a gruelling encounter by all accounts. He told me how he was completely convinced that the local council had put benches along the side of the route in order to try and tempt him to sit down and stop, he believed so hard that this was the case that he used his anger for the council and its benches to push harder towards the finish. I now understand exactly how he felt, all I could think of was why I needed a sign to tell me I still had a long way to go, I knew I still had a long way to go!

On Day 13 I met Kimee Armour, an American Para-Games athlete who I can now say that I have had the pleasure of running alongside. Kimee saw me effectively crawling past her house, read the banners on the RV and felt compelled to come and run with me - our very own Forrest Gump moment. After the normal pleasantries, we continued down the road at which point Kimee turned to me and said, "You do know, you're on the wrong side of the road?" We had travelled over 1,000 miles and no-one had mentioned that I was running on the wrong side of the road. I couldn't help but laugh, could we have looked any more out of place in this foreign land?

Chapter 14

World's Largest Rocking Chair.

After two weeks on the road, you are feeling every emotion possible. Tensions in the RV were high, it was no one's fault, it's just being together every single day, the little things start to get to you and arguments begin to erupt. I blame the road, the road does strange things to your mind. Some days you feel like you could conquer the world, others you feel like an insignificant speck. The worries and panics I had before heading to the US and at the start of the adventure were gone, like most things people worry about, they turned out to be pointless. We had seen so much by this point, we had made countless errors but in doing so we had learnt some incredibly valuable lessons.

The morning of Day 14 we stood in St. Louis at the Gateway Arch, the largest free-standing arch in the world. We had once again beaten the commuters and the streets were quiet. A dark, dank drizzle had settled over the city, but even in the miserable weather, I liked St. Louis.

Navigation throughout the entire trip was a bone of contention for me. Find me a decent route with long roads of unbroken tarmac and I loved you, send me the wrong way and make me climb tortuous hills and you were my worst enemy. Helen agreed to navigate us out of St. Louis and towards the place where we would spend the evening, a town called Doolittle. I don't know if we picked the place by how much we liked the name but this had to be one of my favourites.

I should at this point mention that Helen still holds her hand up in an "L" shape when turning to the left to check which way is left and so, if I'm honest, I was wary of where we might end up. The hard part, navigating out of St. Louis, Helen did with ease, then as the roads opened up the call came over the radio, "TURN LEFT BOATWRIGHT!" It was said with conviction and confidence, who was I to argue? I followed my orders. As I did so, I looked to my right and saw that the road continued to follow the river, gradual easy-riding, flat, almost majestic. I looked to my left, my eyes continuing upwards as the hill in front of me loomed. A pump of the legs and out of the saddle, I attacked the climb with gusto, it was still early and I felt strong, the sponge soaked up any lumps and bumps on the flat and my legs welcomed the rush of adrenaline. It was a good 2.5 mile climb and by the time I got to the top I was heaving for breath and definitely a lot warmer than what I was at the bottom.

The radio crackled in my pocket, "Ermmmmmmmmmmm...... I think we should have turned right" said Helen, I can tell by her tone she is telling me this whilst cowering behind the map. "Sorry, you did really well on that climb though!" I took a massive deep breath and counted to ten (and then ten again and ten again for a third time). A quick glance back and a smile to Helen and the rest of the team, I dipped over the edge of the hill and powered back down the valley. The climb that had taken an age to power up was descended in minutes.

The old route runs parallel to Interstate 44, twisting and turning as it moves across the state, north of the Mark Twain National Forest, we pass towns called St. Clair, Stanton, Bourbon and we rest in Cuba. I loved Cuba because it was nothing like anything we had seen so far on the journey. There were no high street chain shops, or shopping malls. It was full of independent, family-run shops. The devastation caused by the interstate was evident once again. Cuba was lucky - lucky to have people there willing to fight for their livelihoods. Many of the towns we rolled through were ghost towns, this was not through choice, the people there had lost everything. Many times we saw that the tables were still set, the sofa and chairs still there, it looked like one-day people just decided they had had enough and they had upped and left. Where they moved to I have no idea.

After Cuba came a place called Fanning, Missouri, the home of the now second largest rocking chair in the world. The chair was erected on April Fool's day in 2008 outside of the US 66 Outpost and General Store. The chair was built as a way to try and entice people into the store, and I have to say it works!

The riding had been great all day, smooth roads and a minimal amount of climbing, the sponge absorbing the lumps and bumps of the road. Mechanically the bike was doing ok, she had taken some pain over the last two weeks and was starting to creak a little bit but she was doing pretty well all things considered.

Kerry and I at the foot of the giant rocking chair, Fanning, Missouri, Day 14.

My bike was not some Olympic sprint bike or some kind of Tour De France 2-gram mega bike, nope, in fact my bike was a near ten-year-old eBay purchase. My derailleur had bent in transit, my seat stem was held by God only knows what and as soon as I applied a little bit of pressure in certain gears the chain would jump and change gear completely independently but aside from all these things she was perfect. We called her Tallulah. The name is taken from the Bobsled in the film 'Cool Runnings' which sees a group of Jamaican bob-sledders appear at the winter Olympics. They too were considered the underdog and told they could not do what they set out to do, they too wanted to change people's perceptions, and they too sought to triumph over adversity.

Doolittle, Missouri, our goal for the evening, was not what I expected. As there was little to nothing there, we stayed in a truck stop just off the interstate. It wasn't glamourous or pretty, it was a long way from the friends and families houses we had stayed at along the way but for right then, at that moment in time, it was exactly what we needed - a place to rest our weary heads.

Chapter 15

Thanks for picking Uranus.

I remember writing my blog at the end of Day 15 and saying that this day will go down as one that in days, weeks and months to come I would look back and think, "WOW, that was really stupid!" The truth is I don't think that at all, now when I look back and I think about that day, I think "Wow, I ran 62.5 miles (100 km) in one day." I don't look back and think that it was easy but I think that we as a team came together when we needed to. After 150 miles in the sweltering heat (around 30 degrees) the previous day, we had managed to get to a point 62.5 miles from our truck stop in Doolittle. We had arrived in another town called Springfield, this time it was Springfield, Missouri.

The heat and humidity seemed to have crept back in over the previous couple of days, and so once again weight loss was becoming an issue. Humidity equated to more sweat and more sweat meant weight loss. I tried my hardest to control it, I drank every time I came to a stop, choking down hydration salts and anything in liquid form that I could swallow. Yet again, though, it was about finding that balance. Too much liquid and it swished in my stomach and made me feel very sick, not enough and my vision started to blur due to the dehydration.

I got away well in the morning, my legs freeing up and allowing me to get into my stride early. I did not mention to the team my intentions of trying to run 62.5 miles. I thought that if I did mention it they would just try and talk me out of it (and understandably so). I was, at this point, 50 miles behind schedule due to a gruelling day on the bike a few days before but I felt strong and motivated, I knew I could get it done. I worked out in my head that I would break the day up into small manageable blocks of 25 km (15.5 miles). It might sound strange to some people, but to me running in kilometres rather than miles made it sound much less.

Day 15 was not only the day of the 100km but it was also the day that the hills changed. They changed from being a pleasant, gentle, downhill slope to a bone crushing agonising descent which you wouldn't wish on your worst enemy. Uphill affected my heart and lungs but I could control that easily through pace, downhill felt like someone had put red hot pokers through my quad muscles and not only that, they were twisting them.

The day was brutally tough but the team, landscape and towns kept me going. At one point, we saw a sign saying 'Tan your Fanny' and we went through a town called Uranus which had a famous fudge company. The sign here read 'Fudge Made in Uranus'. It still makes me giggle even now. As we left Uranus the leaving sign stated, 'Thanks for picking Uranus' – absolute brilliance. Just like Fanning and its large rocking chair, Uranus are doing something to try and get people to come off the interstate and see them, they are fighting, they are giving it a go. I think that's what the American Dream is to me, people willing to give it a go.

The road was quiet. Grass had begun to grow in some of the cracks to further emphasise this point. Houses on this part of Route 66 were very rare. We arrived at the bottom of a hill where the road bent round and the climb shot straight up a hillside and into the mist, it was called 'The Devil's Elbow', I will never forget it. "Head down and one foot in front of the other!" I chanted to myself as I began the ascent. The top of the climb still shrouded in mist, the trees looming large over the road. As I progressed up the hill the trees gave way to rock faces, you could see how the road had cut through the stone. There were signs scattered all over the cliff face warning of falling boulders. I pushed higher into the mist, my breathing now heavy and laboured, sweat pouring from my brow, leaving a damp trail on the road behind me. "Don't quit, don't quit!" I repeated to myself over and over as I inched up the hill. The mist cleared as I reached the top of the climb, the team were waiting there to greet me with yet more liquid. I sat on the tailgate for a few moments, broken but triumphant, another step closer to the end.

The climb conquered but beyond exhausted.

As I reached the end and the 100km mark I knew I needed to stop, I knew at that point I didn't have much else to give. I'm not sure if you have ever felt like this but my vision didn't move properly as I turned my head, it was like it was in still frames, everything moving in ultra-slow motion. My hearing wasn't clear any more, distorted noises, slow and deep filled my ears, I was struggling to make out shapes and I felt disorientated - had I not known much better I would have said that I was drunk. It was at that point that the team saved me, they brought me back in, rehydrated me and forced horrible concoctions down my throat, whatever it was and whatever they did - it worked.

Some of the team at the Rocky Steps, Philadelphia.

Day 4, Ice bath in a lake.

I think the sign says it all.

The start of Route 66.

Tallulah.

The team at the finish line, Santa Monica Pier.

Chapter 16

Paris Roubaix, in America?

Waking up in an RV was a difficult experience every day. Banging and clanging my way through the RV to the bathroom, the constant battle to put my socks on, the fly paper sticking to my hair and face as I threw myself onto the bed whilst trying to hitch up my running tights. However, one thing I loved was that every day we woke up somewhere different, somewhere new. Sometimes it was a car park others a truck stop and on occasion a layby but wherever it was, it just added to our adventure.

Heading towards Joplin on the bike I knew that by the end of the day I would be over the halfway mark and we were aiming to camp on the border of three states; Missouri, Oklahoma and Kansas. I was still in recovery mode from the 100km run and didn't I know it. Every day as I lay down to sleep my body was tired, it was aching and it needed rest but the true damage wasn't seen until the morning after. This time around, remarkably, the majority of my body was ok. I had the normal aches and pains but this had become the norm to me now, this pain was as natural as breathing in and out, it was just something that was there throughout.

This time there was a different type of pain - my nipples. I have heard many people talk of runner's nipple but it was nothing I had really encountered before and during the 100km it was nothing I was aware of, particularly. On awakening that morning, however, I felt like someone was in the middle of sand papering my nipples off, they were beyond sore even with a soft shirt resting against them. Immediate action was needed before I put on my t-shirt and set off on the bike. This time the sponge couldn't save me so Vaseline did. It was applied by the handful, so much so that a closer look may have suggested a small but developing cleavage.

Once I had got going, a good hour passed before I even saw my first car. We were up and away early, a great start after the torture of the day before. As I passed through the towns, each one had a small sign stating the town you were about to pass and the population. The populations varied along the way, some larger towns of 50,000 people and some with only 150 people. Interspersed between these towns were small holdings, tiny groups of houses or sometimes just one house on its own. I was doing 150 miles every day on my bike and sometimes I would not see a supermarket or grocery store for days. I couldn't help but think to myself, "Where do these people shop? What do they do? Where do they go on Christmas Day?" I just couldn't understand life out there, I am a country boy but even for me this was remote.

At times when at home and life becomes busy and chaotic, we long for that peace and quiet, just something to slow life down a bit, out in the American midwest life doesn't get much slower. The peace and quiet are your friend at first, helping you stay focussed and alert to what might be coming, slowly you realise there is nothing coming, there will only be you, on that road, all day. It's a lonely place out on the road with only your own thoughts to think about. You imagine all the great things you will do when you get home, I imagined what I might do if I managed to finish, what would I say? I cursed myself for thinking about the finish line. "1 day at a time, 1 hour at a time and 1 inch at a time, bloody idiot!" I said to myself.

The hills in Missouri are not like the hills around Yorkshire, in Yorkshire when you climb you are out of the saddle for a while, they keep going, each one testing you a little more than the last. I don't know if it's just me and because I'm a miserable Yorkshireman but I have always believed that there are more uphill's than down in Yorkshire. Missouri's hills lull you into a false sense of security, because as with anywhere in America the roads are so straight that the hills look bigger than they actually are, like a thankfully pleasant optical illusion. Unlike the hills in Yorkshire you don't really have to get out of your seat, if you don't want to. I am a climber who likes to be out of the saddle and pumping my legs, to me that's a personal choice, some will sit down all day. Missouri's hills require just a little more than staying seated all the way to the top but not quite enough to stand up and pump your legs. What it meant for me was that I found the hills very frustrating, by the time I had stood up out of the saddle I was sat back down again within a minute, having already reached the summit of the hill.

As I neared Joplin the road surface deteriorated to the point where it resembled cobblestones. It genuinely looked like a visually challenged individual had laid the tarmac - one patch here, another over there, paving slab here, some gravel over there. There was nothing uniform and it was absolutely horrible to cycle over. I can only imagine that this is what it must be what it is like to cycle the Paris Roubaix (for those not in the know, this is a cycle race on cobblestones). My hands, wrists, elbows and back were beaten to bits, opening or more accurately prising my hands off of the handle bars was painful. My jaw hurt so much it felt like I had been chewing the same piece of gum for the last 20 years. I could barely talk, grit had built up between my teeth because they had been constantly grinding together. I needed to rest.

They always say it's much harder for you to tell if you have lost weight - other people will tell you all the time that you look thin or you look fat, in fact, they are more than happy to point these things out but it is difficult to see it on yourself. It wasn't until well into the trip that I started to notice the changes with regards to my body. The scales will tell you that you have lost weight but physically I couldn't see it, however, after 16 days I was beginning to see the changes. My chest and arms could only be described as mush, like the muscle in them was just melting away. My arms had lost definition and seemed to be one straight line from my wrist to my arm pit. The strange thing about it was, there was nothing I could do to stop this – it was inevitable on this adventure.

Day 16 finished without any further episodes, we stopped and rested just outside of Joplin.

Day 17 - a running day - saw us cross into the great state of Oklahoma. We crossed the state line at a place called Seneca, it was unbelievably warm and very muggy. In Britain, we would say that it 'needs to break', there was a strange feeling of pressure in the weather. I felt like I was running with an extra layer of clothing on. It was 32 degrees but felt closer to 50, I couldn't take deep breaths, as I felt as if I was suffocating just when I was breathing in.

After 10 miles of running, I stopped. This wasn't normal. Usually, I was powering through a half marathon or occasionally a full marathon before I took a break. I stopped on the banks of a lake; it was called 'Grand Lake o' the Cherokees', a beautifully majestic place, buzzing with wildlife. I stared at the water, perfectly still and calm; it was mesmerizing, just the sheer size of the lake was breath-taking. The bridge we had crossed to get across the lake was larger than most I had seen in Britain and, yet, this was on a quiet, country highway. Having stood for what felt like hours I turned to carry on, I glanced back only to see that I had created a lake of my own where I had been standing.

We passed the small towns of Wyandotte and Fairland during the morning session. The heat unerringly increasing, becoming more and more intense as the day went on. Up until this day, I had been running 6 miles in about an hour, on Day 17 this took me 1 hour and 40 minutes. I was barely moving when the sun was at its strongest.

There was nothing pleasant about Day 17, I was hot, tired and feeling like the world was against me. The scenery was not helping, the roads were straight and there was the occasional bridge but that was about it. Absurdly, I longed for a hill - I wanted anything to take away the mind-numbing monotony of where I was.

Towards the end of the day when thoroughly knackered, I came to one of the toughest tests on the road - dogs. You can take being barked at, you can accept dogs on leads moving towards you or even dogs attached to kennels by chains trying to chase you, but dogs on the road side was a brand new experience for me. I love dogs - I have a dog - but I was in Hillbilly heaven and I am not sure that these dogs had seen anyone in the last 10 years. Turns out I can run pretty fast when I need to, my mileage went from 12 minute miles to 5 minute miles very quickly. The dogs were very quick but once I was out of the territory, they stopped chasing me. I felt sick once the adrenalin had subsided. Pain lathered my body, my heart beat faster than it had in days. Those dogs were nearly responsible for ending the 'Epic Adventure'.

Kerry helping me at the end of another long day.

Lack of sleep is a killer. It clouds your judgement, it effects your ability to complete simple tasks but most of all when working in a team it makes you incredibly short tempered and unwilling to accept any other point of view but your own. Stopping in Vinita, Oklahoma was the toughest night of my life, the temperature never dropped from the level it had attained during the day. The tiny air-conditioning unit of the RV struggled unsuccessfully to cool the RV. The warm, stagnant, sweaty air wafted backwards and forwards up and down the RV. We were camped in a Walmart car park for the evening, entering the supermarket and standing in the freezer aisle just to cool down. I could easily have got in and slept with the fish fingers. Lying in bed that night, sweat poured from my head, the tiny desk fan we had bought just shoved the warm air round the room. Any movement of my body produced a wave of sweat, saturating into my pillow. Sleep, once again, unsurprisingly eluded me. I lay all night, as still as possible, praying for just 5 minutes of sleep, but my prayers were not answered.

As the sun came up, I got up. Every morning I checked my messages - the messages of support were overwhelming. They made each day that tiny bit easier and this was especially necessary after a night of little to no sleep. As I got out of my sweat-soaked bed on Day 18, I had a message from my younger brother, always a man with beautiful words. I read it before I set off on the bike. All the way across I had said to myself, "Don't let pain break you." I quoted motivational lines from films and all the clichéd inspirational quotes that you see on social media. In the end pain didn't break me, it couldn't, but this message from my brother, Luke, did:

I have just spoken to Sam Boatwright through the magic of FaceTime and I am now more in awe of him than ever.

For me, I just think of when I am tired and hurting. I think about how at these times the little things like perhaps the noise of insects or the heat of the sun can/ could drive me insane, even at home. However, after just talking to my brother I realise how mentally tough he is, how his incredible sense of humour enables him to make everything seem trivial and how this helps him to deal with all the difficulties he is being faced with.

Sam may not be superhuman in terms of his physical attributes - he works incredibly hard to be as fit as he is - but Sam is definitely a superhuman in terms of mentality because how can you possibly prepare for the torment, the challenge, the sheer exhaustion that he faces everyday?

I do not know and probably will never know how you do it bruv but I will spend my life telling people about your achievements and making sure they know just how proud I am to share my name with you.

So people please give my brother every bit of support that you can - like his page, share his posts and most importantly donate to Help for Heroes. This man, my brother, runs for those who can't - all we have to do is help him along the way, it's not too much to ask, is it? #epicadventure #smilingbig #helpforheroes

Chapter 17

Commando Crawling in Oklahoma

We had had a team meeting on the evening of Day 17, we needed a different approach for the rest of the trip as the heat was becoming too much. It was brutal, gruelling work and we needed to do something different. We decided that the something different was rising an hour earlier and being on the road before 6am. It sounds quite early to be getting up at 4.45am and having breakfast, but we couldn't sleep anyway because of the heat, why not get the day started?

It was 25 degrees at 6am; we had stayed in a Walmart car Park next to the rodeo on the edge of Vinita. Farmers and animals were milling around the local auction, life for people of Vinita was hard, and farming seemed to be the main income for the locals. The town reminded of my hometown of Skipton; the auction, the quaint little shops and the high street at the centre. It was a lovely little town.

The day whizzed by in a blur of monumental heat, cornfields and straight roads. We passed towns like Chelsea, Foyil, Claremore and Catoosa. Foyil being home of the world's largest totem pole. It was 30 degrees by 10am but it was calm and peaceful, the roads were relatively quiet and Tallulah and the sponge absorbed the majority of the bumps and cracks of the road. Just after 10am and a good morning's cycling we stopped in Tulsa for a bite to eat. For a while I just stared at my meal, it wasn't that I couldn't eat it, but I had just become completely overwhelmed by how far we had come and how well the team had done. I knew we had come a long way, not because of the way my body felt or because the maps said so. I knew because in the sitcom 'Friends', Chandler takes a job in Tulsa, and they agree, it's a long way from New York City.

A few days before we arrived in Tulsa, the city had been hit by a tornado, 7 people had been hospitalized from this, a major reminder of where were and what the weather in America could do if you were in the wrong place at the wrong time. It was strange to be sat down for our lunch at 10am but I was hungry and needed the fuel. The heat was still energy sapping even in the early morning and this was coupled with a significant lack of sleep.

We spent the night of Day 18 camped on the banks of Arcadia Lake, a little north of Oklahoma City near a town called Edmond. On this night, Arcadia Lake became my giant ice bath. I waded out and fell gently backwards into the water, totally immersed in the cold of the lake, I could immediately feel the swelling in my muscles begin to retreat. The cold water washed the sweat from my body, I half expected steam to rise from my baking skin as I hit the water. The team joined me. It was a brilliant way to finish a successful day on the bike. The entire team sat in a lake, in Oklahoma.

Day 18 had passed almost entirely without incident, this was in stark contrast to what was about to come on Day 19. Over the next four days, I had to do two running days back to back followed by two bike days back to back. The reason behind this was that the next member of our team (Darren, Helen's husband) was joining us for the final push. He would be landing at Oklahoma airport which is on the outskirts of Oklahoma City. We were already on the northern outskirts of the city. As such, if I had cycled, we would have ended up 200 miles from the airport which would have meant a long round trip to collect him and this seemed ridiculous. We had, therefore, made the decision as a team that I should do back to back days of running and then cycling.

As 3am came around, just like in Pittsburgh, our mobile phones vibrated and beeped in unison, but this time it was followed by what can only be described as a military style air raid siren. "WARNING, WARNING, WARNING!" exclaimed a robotic voice over the public address system, "THIS IS A STATE WEATHER WARNING!" It continued to describe the weather that was due to hit Oklahoma imminently. Thunder, lightning rain and high winds were due for the area. Rain blasted and pelted the RV, throughout the night, lightning crashed into the trees around the RV Park and like a bass drum keeping beat the thunder boomed continually for hours. Sleep once again evaded the team.

We rose early the next morning with sleep deprivation in full swing. Kerry ran with me first thing, she enjoyed the early morning running, it helped get her up and about and set her up for the day. Helen joined me after a few miles and we pressed on towards Oklahoma

City. It was one of the larger cities we had passed for a while and so we knew that the RV would struggle to stay near us. We made a plan for the RV to drive a little way further up the road and then we would run to it each time and we would continue through the city like that.

Helen and I weaved through the streets of Oklahoma. It was warm and muggy but raining at the same time - a dangerous combination as you are completely unaware of how much sweat is coming out of you. Avoiding floods from the previous night's deluge was impossible, often our only option was to run through the flood or dice with danger and run into the road. We were already wet so the flood tended to be the clearest and most sensible option.

Each time Helen and I were running we were searching for the RV. We knew that when we reached it we could rest - we could have a break. Now I must inform you that the streets in Oklahoma City (much like the rest of America) are in straight lines and once you are on one street you can stay on it for miles and it won't change. What this should also mean is that it is nearly impossible to lose anyone or anything on these roads.

On one such road, we ran and ran and ran and ran, yet, we could not find the RV. We discussed the road we were on and agreed that we were headed in the right direction but we could not locate the RV. We were sure we were in the right place. "How could anyone get lost on a straight road?" We kept saying to each other. I was losing my temper very quickly, the RV had to have gone wrong, we weren't going fast enough to get lost.

The weather had been so bad at the start, that neither of us could carry a mobile phone as it would have flooded within the first 2 minutes, this was now proving to have been a poor decision.

We crested a small climb and as we did, we saw that the smaller roads now merged with what looked like the start of the M1! The lanes went from single carriage to a 4 lane interstate, we were stuck. At the other side of the interstate were some car garages, risking death or at the very least severe injury we crossed the interstate. This would be the first of two interstate crossings that day, neither of which I would like to experience again.

No money, no phone and no water we pulled into the Hyundai Garage in Oklahoma City. Like drowned rats we stood in the foyer, water dripping onto the floor all around us, it looked like we had swum to the garage. Approaching the very loud woman at reception, Helen asked if we could use the phone – the only issue being that we didn't know anyone else's number! Luckily the power of social media came to our aid, we messaged Kerry telling her where we were and added our location - this was followed by a lot of exclamation marks!

When I ran in 2012, my own mother had managed to do the something very similar. In the small Scottish town of Montrose, she had managed to completely miss the large, ginger-bearded runner resembling her son coming passed the front of the campervan, as she was reading the newspaper. Strangely it hammered down with rain all day that day as well, "I was reading the paper!" she said as she caught me up 5 miles down the road, a huge smile on her face and wiping tears of laughter from her eyes.

We were running hard out of Oklahoma City, some stretches the team joined me for and for others I was left alone. We were heading towards a small town called Bethany. Helen once again running with me, Kerry inside the RV navigating. We then hit a section where it said 'Road ahead closed'. The RV had no chance of passing, "I'm sure we will get through on the pavement!" I said to the guys at a little meeting on the side of the road. The RV set off in the opposite direction, agreeing to meet us on the other side of the roadworks, a few streets up. It disappeared into the distance and we set off towards where it said that the road was closed. As we approached the team working on the road, we realised why the road was shut. The bridge that had previously spanned the interstate was not there, two thin walls crossed the interstate and in between them was just a massive hole. I looked to Helen, "Sh$t!" was the best word that I could muster.

We looked up and down the street and saw a small gap in the fence which lead down to the interstate - another potentially risky crossing. In fact, it was worse this time as there wasn't an island in the middle where we could wait. On other side of the interstate stood a tall concrete banking with a large steel fence at the top. We passed under the fence and stood at our side of the interstate, cars whizzed by, there were 8 lanes to cross in order to get to the other side. In hindsight this was stupid, not just due to the 8 lanes of traffic but mainly because we had not actually worked out how to get up the banking once we got to the other side. At a small gap in the traffic we ran; sprinting, screaming and shrieking like little girls as we crossed the interstate. Our hearts were still pounding and we were breathless as we reached the other side still alive. At this point we looked up, really for the first time, at the daunting, concrete slope in front of us. We walked up and down the side of the interstate for a while looking for a gap. We found a small storm drain. The drain moved the water from the streets above down the ramp and into the sewage system below. Dropping to our bellies, we commando-crawled through the mud and slime up the storm drain eventually appearing from under the fence onto the street above. 2000 miles we had covered and we were crawling up a storm drain in Oklahoma. Our small mercy was that the rain had stopped so there wasn't water pouring down the drain on to us as we climbed up.

Chapter 18

Well, That's Very British

At the end of Day 20, I had completed 1853.5 miles or to anyone else a really, really long way. The John O'Groats to Land's End challenge in 2015 seemed like a very long time ago, and the failures that accompanied that challenge were being put to bed. I had doubled the distance of that challenge and I wasn't finished yet.

In the animated children's film 'Cars', they describe how the interstate cuts through the heart of the country, ploughing a line of destruction across America. The businesses and people are left by the wayside, forgotten about because like with anything nowadays we want something faster. The old highway dips and corkscrews across the country, it meanders with the land and rivers, romantically flowing its way through small towns and villages. There are so many of the towns and villages boarded up, closed down and moved on. We stopped on Day 20 at an old petrol station; we took a picture in the pouring rain. A beautiful old fuel pump, the inside of the shop still decorated with Route 66 memorabilia. What made this particularly sad was that the interstate was just a matter of yards away but no slip road had been created to get to this village. In order to get there, you would have to come off of the interstate a few miles away. You have to accept that no-one would do this ordinarily. The business had no chance.

Kerry and I ran most of the morning, the weather was very British – it was raining from the moment we set off and then continually for the next 12 hours. To pass the time, I would often count different things on the road; sometimes it might be people, cars, cows or even houses, on this day we counted dead frogs, they were everywhere. It seemed we were running on a burial ground for the brave little amphibians that had dared to try to cross the highway. More than likely, they died of shock at the fact that there was even a car on these desolate and isolated roads. Once again weeds had begun to spring up through the gaps in the tarmac, I'm sure it won't be long before the road in this area is gone forever and the only option available to people is the interstate.

Kerry and I at one of the many abandoned fuel pumps on Route 66.

I plundered on through the day, avoiding the large floods where I could but, in the end, I was soddened and soaked to the bone. Helen joined me again for a little run and as she did a procession of Harley Davidsons came passed us, waving and beeping as they followed the mother road, a brilliant and quite surreal sight. No people had passed us for hours, but as the rain leaked off of the end of my nose, I stood, shorts on and wearing a now see-through formerly white t-shirt, as over 50 motorcycles passed, each one a different wave, nod or beep – it was brilliant.

As you travel further west the local people seem to make more of a big deal of Route 66, there is more signage, more touristy stuff for people to look at and a lot more things to do. We passed through Hydro, Weatherford and Clinton - all of which have museums and monuments dedicated to Route 66. It's a big deal to so many people in these smaller towns, it's their life and their business. I don't work for the American Tourist Board but I implore you, I urge you to get off your bike, get out of your car and go and see these people. They are fantastic, amazing and brilliantly resilient people, who want nothing more than to welcome you into their homes and into their businesses.

Finishing Day 20 concluded two full days of running, I was now faced with two days of cycling and 300 miles to catch me back up. The previous couple of days had been more pleasant with regards to temperature and so some sleep was had, it had been desperately needed.

I lay on the seat in the RV, drifting in and out of consciousness as we whizzed back to Oklahoma City and the airport to pick Darren up. It had been two weeks since we had had another person on the RV; we were all in need of some new conversation. I imagine all Darren wanted to do was sleep; instead we ambushed him and hammered him with 70 different conversations at once.

I love to watch people at the airport, there is never any hate, it is probably some of the purest emotion you will see. We walked towards the gate and as we did we saw Darren. Helen's walk went from a steady controlled pace to a full scale sprint, she leapt at Darren. Smiles and kisses covered their faces, true love.

The RV, now with a team of 5, headed back to where we had finished in Clinton. We parked at the side of the railway, a thoroughly underwhelming location for Darren's first night on the RV. Dogs barked, trains rolled passed and what we now believe to be gun shots continued into the night. The sleep we all needed was once again hard to come by.

Chapter 19

Show Me the Way to Amarillo

We arrived in Texas. British people are told a lot about Texas by the press. We are told about the people and the certain views they have regarding race, religion and even politics. Due to these headlines, I think we headed into Texas was a tinge of trepidation. As with many things on this adventure our perceptions were changed by what we saw and experienced. Texas is a state full of beauty, its vast plains stretch to the horizon and cattle move in swatches across the land - it is truly amazing to see. I remember thinking to myself that you could probably set off in almost any direct and I doubt that you would see another soul all day.

I was at the start of two days of back to back cycling and so I had 300 miles to cover. The pace was fast and my legs were pumping hard to keep my average speed up. Landscapes whizzed by in a blur, blending from one to the next. The roads were a patch work of smooth, bowling-green tarmac and rough, cobbled country lane. The main problem with this was that these changes in surface could happen either within a few feet or a few miles of each other. This made it very hard for me to find any rhythm.

There wasn't much to look at on the bike, the main view I had was the peak of my helmet or the droplet of sweat that accumulated on the tip of my nose. There was a scattering of houses every now and again, the occasional small outpost shop selling the very bare essentials but, aside from this, all you could see were fields – just fields.

We passed through a few different little towns; Erick, Sayre, Texola and Mclean. Mclean was my favourite - it was virtually abandoned but there was still a faint pulse resonating around the town. We pulled into Mclean towards the back end of the day. The majority of shops were closed and looked like they had been for a while, buildings were falling down or had already been pulled down and there was hardly anyone around.

The town was built in 1909 by an English Rancher, who died in 1912 aboard the Titanic. As we headed towards the south side of the town we saw a woman parked in the middle of the road staring at one of the torn down buildings. She wound her window down and greeted us. After the normal pleasantries and the usual shock at why we happened to be stood in Mclean on this particular day at this particular town, she began to tell us all about the history of the town. She told us tales of the town with great passion but also great sadness. The building she was staring at was the old cinema, it had been demolished the day before we arrived in Mclean. She told us of the antique shop she used to run and how vibrant and busy the town used to be. As we parted company the woman turned to me and asked me what my favourite part of America had been so far. "That's easy," I said, a little smile coming to my face, "the people!"

Each time that I have undertaken a challenge it has always been the people that have helped me. It has been the kindness of strangers, it has been the beep of a horn or the cheer of passing people. America was no different - like any place it has its problems, where doesn't? However, at its core America believes in its Dream, and to me, that's all that matters.

The humidity of Oklahoma was left well behind. We were now pushing towards the desert and dry heat. The temperature had stuck at a steady 30 degrees for the majority of the day, the skies had been a clear blue with only the odd dab of white cloud.

We stopped in Amarillo that evening, and we probably sang the famous Tony Christie song about 40,000 times during that evening. The RV site was nice, large and flat with hundreds of other RVs rested up alongside ours. As tea cooked and we all set about our own little jobs on the RV, the weather warning system went again. The clouds drew in and lightning cracked down in the distance lighting up the sky with every bolt. The air was different this time, to the storms earlier in the trip, this time the wind swirled as if a tornado was forming. Now, as much as I was excited to see a tornado I really was not keen on one appearing above our RV. As you can imagine, our nerves were a tiny bit frayed as the immense storm began to accumulate above us. The storm last two hours – but we survived.

The following day the sun broke through early, the clouds were gone and the sky was clear blue. However, the wind that so quickly whisked the storm up had stuck around, it was clearly not going to be pleasant on the bike. Pushing out that morning the wind channelled straight at me. It was back-breaking work keeping an average speed. It had been a while since the head wind had been this fierce and I was struggling. After an hour in the saddle, I pulled to the side of the road. I needed to speak with the team about a strategy, something we could do in order to get the mileage in. At my current pace, it would take about 17 hours to get the 150 miles done. The surface we were on was ok, a few potholes here and there but nothing that would throw me off the bike. We decided the best solution was for me to draft off of the RV. If you don't know what this is, this is what happens in the peloton during the Tour De France – it is why they always cycle in a big group. The RV provides protection from the wind resistance, it is scientifically proven and it worked! Behind the RV I conserved more energy and I was able to go a little faster with less effort. I powered along at a great pace (for a bike), the RV trundled along in front.

Just outside Amarillo is the Cadillac Ranch - a freakishly contemporary piece of art work where cars are buried half way into the Earth. Tourists are invited to go and spray-paint their names on to the old cars and have their photos taken. It was quite cool to see these cars just stuck in the middle of a cornfield, there doesn't seem to be any rhyme or reason as to why it's done like this. It's freaky but also somewhat beautiful.

It was whilst reflecting on this artwork that I became aware of one very embarrassing thing. I had left my sponge in. It looked like I had pooed a brick. I also realised that I had done this every time that I had gotten off of my bike since the sponge's introduction. I now wonder what everyone thought when they saw me, most wouldn't have a clue what I was doing. They would have seen a large, pasty individual who had dressed in Lycra and then seemingly soiled himself and was subsequently walking about in this state – I make quite an impression on my travels.

Kerry and I at the Cadillac Ranch, Magic Sponge on show. Amarillo, Route 66.

We moved into New Mexico at great pace, the heat pushing towards 32 degrees, baking me as I pedalled. It baffled my mind that I had just cycled through a time zone, surely that only happens when you go on holiday? All I could think about was what if you lived in one time zone and worked in another, that must be incredibly confusing.

New Mexico could be its own country – it was very different. The Earth there was scorched red from the baking sun and the rivers were a dirty, reddy-brown colour. Everything and everyone just looked too hot, even the cows. I, evidently, was no exception. New Mexico seemed almost lifeless, the desperation of towns we had seen all the way along continued into New Mexico. Ghost towns lay all along the old road, lifeless towns crying out for some sort of civilisation.

It was so hot I stripped down to just my bib shorts in New Mexico. This picture is taken not far from our rest area at Tucumcari on Route 66.

Chapter 20

Walter White Was Right to Choose Here

We had spent the night at a small RV site in the little town of Tucumcari - a bleak place, baked by the constant beating of the sun's rays. Everything looked cooked and frazzled, scorched from hours every day in direct sun light. Like a few towns further west, Tucumcari tries to create some sort of nostalgia about the Mother Road. They have paintings on the pavement, museums dedicated to the route and many of the motels are named after something from the route. I couldn't help but think that living things do well to survive out there.

I ran out of the town early; our morning regime would continue until the end of the trip now. The heat at 6am was quite pleasant, nowhere near the temperatures of the early afternoon. At home, even at 6am the traffic would be building, people would be rushing for trains and buses, cars would be whizzing by, everyone would be in a rush. Out there, there is no rushing, what would they be rushing for? It is still, stagnant and lifeless.

I ran for 4 hours solid and saw 8 cars on the old Route 66. The road was in a shocking state of disrepair and once again, like other parts earlier in the trip, the weeds were winning, you could tell that it wouldn't be long before this part of the road gave up. I would normally list all the towns we went through and the different architecture or touristy things that we saw – we saw nothing, nothing but arid land, cacti, some rocks and a lot of red dirt.

Everyone ran with me on this day, it was nice for them to be able to stretch their legs, as well. After two days cooped up on the RV, we needed a change of pace, we needed fresh air and some different conversation. It's amazing what you talk about when you're out on the road, it's like your very own therapy session. For some reason, you feel more inclined to open up to people about the things going on in your life, the problems you might have or the worries you're facing. It could be because you feel like you now share some special bond but it was the same when I did my first run. People would come and join me and within minutes they were telling me everything about themselves. I would always listen and give advice where possible but most of the time I think people just wanted to talk, I was happy enough to listen. We spoke about anything and everything from politics to fridge magnets.

The heat in New Mexico was different than anything I had experienced earlier, it wasn't wet and muggy instead it was dry - unbelievably dry. My clothes were not wet with sweat at the end of the day, instead they were bone dry and dusty. My sweat dripped from my forehead onto my hand and by the time it touched my hand it had turned to salt, it was brilliant and frightening at the same time. Hydration was going to be even more important as I neared the finish and it was now much harder to detect when I needed hydrating.

One thing I had not taken into account when planning this trip was altitude. Call it a blip or a rookie mistake, whatever you want to call it, I had absolutely no idea that along with the blistering heat, the running and the cycling that I would also have to deal with altitude. It was hard enough trying to breath in the dustbowl that was New Mexico, but to make matters worse the air was now going to be thinner!

I muttered to myself as I stomped along the road having passed a sign saying' Welcome to Santa Rosa – 5000 feet above sea level'. Luckily for us Santa Rosa was where we were stopping that evening, I was shattered and now heavily heaving for air.

As we sat on the RV that evening I knew that there was more climbing to come and that the air would get even thinner. I looked at the maps, searching for as much information as I could find about the area. One part of the route kept coming up, The Continental Divide. I had no idea what it was or for that matter where it was, I just knew from the research we had just done that it was going to be a slog to get there.

As I looked out over New Mexico, I now realised why Walter White chose this place to cook his Crystal Meth - there is no one here and those that are here can't move because they can't breathe. It's ideal for illegal activity, no one could or would chase you.

Chapter 21

Albuquerque, I just like to say the word

Day 24 was a great day in the saddle, the roads were long and wide with near perfect tarmac. The sponge was still lodged in place and cushioned me as I drafted off of the RV, maintaining an average speed of 30 miles per hour almost all day. When cruising at these sorts of speeds your days become shorter, life becomes easier and everyone is smiling. The faster I could go, the quicker the team were able to get off the RV.

Drafting, however, is challenging. I needed everyone to be working as a unit in order to make it work effectively. I stayed about 6 inches off of the back bumper of the RV, a horrible and dangerous place to be. I couldn't see what was coming up and traffic behind me didn't always realise that we were going pretty slowly. On occasion cars came screeching to a halt behind me, this is according to the team, thankfully I couldn't see this happening!

The team sat on the bed at the back of the RV looking out of the back window at me, the driver at the front could not see me at all. The communication was kept very simple - thumbs up meant that I wanted to go faster, thumbs down meant that I needed to slow down and OK meant that we needed to stay as we were. It worked very well for the majority of the day, the RV almost pulled me up some of the smaller climbs. The only time our communications let us down a little bit was when I was going very fast downhill and I felt like I was going to plough into the back of the RV or when I was going up a long climb and I couldn't quite keep up with the RV.

As much as I loved going fast and eating up the mileage, 6 inches off the back of the RV is a nasty, dusty and incredibly warm place to be. Dirt from the road is constantly flicked into your face, the air is think and warm and no air can get into the little vacuum that the RV creates. The next problem is that if you drop back from 6 inches to three feet, the wind hits you like a punch in your chest and before you know it you are 20 feet further behind the RV using a lot of energy to catch back up to the RV. It was very much a trial and error situation - sometimes we could cover 30-40 minutes of no problems and at other times we would be having near death experiences every 2 minutes.

The route had taken us back closer to civilisation, back somewhere close to what you might call 'normal', although, the landscape was anything but normal. From my position tucked in tight behind the RV I could see nothing in front of me apart from the back window of the RV, but when I looked to my side I was awes-struck, sometimes forgetting that I still had to pedal. The arid, red dirt had given way to rolling mountains, salt flats and the plains of America. Acre after acre of breath-taking unbroken land, no buildings or telegraph poles, no tur-bines or motorways - the landscape was heavenly.

Willard, Vaughn, Chillini and Tijeras were a few of the towns we journeyed through before descending into Albuquerque. As we arrived into Albuquerque, I crested a large climb, the city was sitting beneath me. I could see right across the huge city and off into the distance. The city looked like someone had gathered it up and just placed it haphazardly into the middle of the desert. There are no other towns or cities on the horizon, it is seemingly cut off from the rest of America. Off in the distance before the land met the sky on the horizon you could see yet more desert, an empty vastness. The idea of being cast out of the city and told to walk into the unknown as a form of punishment shoots through my mind.

I descend in to the city, whizzing down the hill at pace, I keep up with the motorised traffic. As we near the centre of town, we call it a day.

A good day on the bike.

Chapter 22

The Continental Divide

Day 25 - I can easily say this was the hardest running day of my life, nothing from the first run even comes close. The hills of Scotland and the valleys of Wales fall a long way short of how I felt by the end of Day 25. They say 'to every Ying there is a Yang', and Day 25 was certainly someone balancing out my days. The euphoria of the day before was replaced by searing pain in my legs and my lungs silently screaming as the air continued to get thinner and thinner. I knew we had been climbing a lot, but now the facts actually backed this up. By the end of the day, we had climbed to a total altitude of 7,245 feet above sea level.

There were, however, a few things that helped to settle my mind - one was knowing that if I had come all this way up then I must be heading down at some point, another was that if I could make it through this day then there would be little I couldn't conquer for the rest of the journey and the final thing that gave me some solace in my agony was knowing that going down the hills on my bike was going to be a lot more fun than running up them.

The heat was still unbelievably intense as we moved out of Albuquerque that morning, heading towards a place called Laguna. It wasn't the energy sapping heat of the mid-day sun, but for 5.30am it was ridiculously warm.

Setting out that morning I scanned the horizon, I did this every day, whether on the bike or running to see if I could picture what the day might bring. As I looked out, all I could see were mountains. We were in what looked like a basin, all around us in one huge circle were mountains. For even the most optimistic of people this would have been tough to take - my heart sank a little.

I don't know whether it's because when you look back at your day you don't remember the easy parts or just because that day there were just no easy sections, but the first 25 miles seemed like a constant uphill battle. Yes, that's right - just a mile short of a marathon without one downhill section. Each step of the ascent, the air got thinner, each minute that the day progressed the temperature increased. It was brutal and unforgiving attack on my senses. I was running as well as could be expected, my lungs were straining at the extra workload my body was asking of them, I felt like a 90 year old asthmatic. Every single member of the team ran with me on Day 25, but each of them could only manage a couple of miles at a time. They jumped on and off the RV like a conveyer belt; a production line of runners. Conversation was down to grunts and head nods with the odd hand gesture thrown in for good measure. I was glad that the team experienced this as well, they understood what was happening to me and why I was finding the day so hard, that empathy was important to me.

The climbing finally came to end, a punishing, gruelling day which I never want to experience again. Kerry ran the last half a mile with me, the signs had ticked down from 10 miles all the way down to when we reached the Continental Divide. The Continental Divide is the point at which water flows in different directions, at one side the water flows to the Pacific Ocean, at the other side the water flows to the Atlantic. As I approached the top of the climb my eyes filled with tears, I had done it, we were at the highest point we would climb to on the journey. Pain flooded through my body but it didn't matter, I collapsed onto Kerry, broken and exhausted. I hobbled and limped to the sign of The Continental Divide. We sat and posed for the obligatory tourist photos, I sat and stared off into the distance, a slight smile cracking at the corner of my mouth, "You did it Sam," I said quietly to myself, "you can be proud of that."

While I rested at the top, I was greeted by a number of different people, all of whom were congratulating me on my achievements so far and wishing me luck for the rest of the trip. One well-wisher was an Australian bloke, an ex-serviceman who was now a police officer and who, along with his buddies, was making his way across Route 66 by motorcycle. In a vice like grip, he shook my hand, "Thank you for what you are doing." he said with passion and emotion in his voice. It was times like that when I realised that what I was doing did make a difference to other people's lives.

I have no idea what got me through that Day. Even now, looking back, I still don't know why or how I kept moving. The number one question I am asked about my running is, how do I keep going day after day? The answer? The answer is - I have no idea. If I did, I think I would be a very rich man. I have often wondered, is it competitiveness? Pride? Drive? Or maybe a mixture of all of these things? When I finished running after the first 'Epic Run' I was asked by all most every child aged between 5 and 11, "Why don't I run in the Olympics?" Apparently, I would destroy Mo Farrah. As much as this would be a brilliant achievement, I have to let you down kids. I won't be beating Mo Farrah any time soon or running in the Olympics. The main reason for this is that I don't run fast, I just know that whatever comes my way I can keep running. Running for me is a chance to discover, to explore to unleash that inner child in me that just wanted to climb trees and dig holes. Somewhere along the way we lose that person, we move away from those dreams and real life takes over. So what if I told you to listen to the 8 year old you? We are going on an adventure where we run and bike across America, what do think the 8 year old you would say?

Kerry and I at The Continental Divide.

Chapter 23

The Ar$e End of Nowhere

Another state line was crossed, and so we were yet another state line closer to the finish. Arizona was the penultimate state - we were getting close. Throughout the trip I had been sent messages about the various different sections that I needed to be careful in, Arizona was the one that came up in most messages, magnificent yet deadly seemed to be the common theme. Looking back at the day now, I am glad we made the decisions we made but at the time tensions were extremely high on the RV.

We galloped out of Gallup (I have been wanting to write that since I began writing this book). Riding well with my average speed pushing towards 32 miles per hour mark. I, once again, stuck closely behind the RV and we were belting out the miles. I was singing every song at the top of my lungs as the early morning sun peaked over the mountains. I was sailing through Arizona; mountains loomed off in the distance as we contoured our way along the valley floor, the odd little rise forcing me out of the saddle and into a standing attack but nothing that I hadn't dealt with before and the draft of the RV pulled me up the lesser climbs.

We were deep in Navajo territory, and if the signs weren't evidence enough, the huge cave paintings were a good indication of where you were. The cliffs and caves continued for an age. When I was a kid my Grandad would sit in his chair and watch John Wayne westerns on an afternoon, this place took me back to my childhood, and I became lost in a world of Cowboys and Indians.

Yet, the nostalgia and enjoyment didn't last long. Suddenly, there was a massive thump on my back wheel, followed by a loud bang – I had hit a cattle grid at 32 miles per hour. As I disembarked, I could see that the tyre was clinging limply to the wheel, it was burst and broken, and the wheel had a large chunk missing from it, as well. This meant that no matter how many tyres or inner tubes we tried, there was no immediate fix, the wheel itself was broken.

It was now where the tensions began to grow; we had a decision to make. My idea was for me to run for the next part whilst the rest of the team travelled the 120 miles to the next town called Show-Low and got the bike fixed. However, I was quickly reminded of my day previously at the Continental Divide (difficulties breathing, etc) and also the day the team had gone to Pittsburgh and how long it had taken them to do that round trip (around about half a day). Arguments for and against flew around the van, in the end, though, common sense overcame bravado. We decided we would load up the bike and the whole team and head to the little town of Show- Low, 120 miles in the wrong direction.

We arrived in Show-Low and after a few brief discussions with the locals about where the bike repair shop was, we found it. They were genuinely incredibly helpful and they began working to get the bike fixed. We decided to have lunch in Show-Low. I munched down an all you can eat pizza buffet in record time – it was all about the very necessary calories. The rest of the team had one or two slices, I had around eight.

We made the decision that, in order to get the miles in, we should cycle back from Show-Low the 120 mile route we had just done in the RV. As we left, we asked the bike shop owner why there were signs warning of snow. He told us that in the winter they get about three to four feet of snow on average. It was 33 degrees and I could not understand how in the world there would ever be snow, I was sweating just standing still. The shop owner was a keen cyclist himself and he reinforced the decision to cycle back towards Route 66 informing me that the wind would be at my back and apparently even he could average about 29 miles per hour himself across some of that route – this proved to be excellent advice.

We pressed back out of Show-Low. The road was a great surface, a well-used highway with trucks rumbling their way along throughout the day. It felt a little too calm and we all felt it was about time we had another brush with the law. Luckily, just then the police pulled us over for holding up the traffic. Sergeant Rush was the name of this police officer, there had been 11 in total so far on the journey. Nearly every officer that had pulled us over had done it purely out of curiosity rather than because we were actually breaking the law. However, on this occasion we were told in explicit detail why and how we were breaking the law. After what felt like an eternity he allowed us to continue. He had one stipulation, though. The RV must travel ahead and not block traffic, we, of course, agreed.

We passed the small towns of Snowflake, Taylor and Holbrook while making our way back the 120 miles we had come, checking all the time that we were not holding up the traffic – we didn't want to be breaking the law, again! The police throughout the trip had been brilliant, in most towns and in every state the police had come to see what we were doing. Sometimes they were worried we had broken down or that I was in distress (I was) but each time they left us with their best wishes and a thank you for what we were doing for our injured veterans.

As we pulled into the Winslow, our finish for the evening, I couldn't help but think how little there was there. If it was in Yorkshire, it would have been called 'The Ar$e End of Nowhere'. There was nothing there at all. We stayed just outside the town centre in a small RV park. The RV park was not manned; it was a self-service place, where you left money in a little tin as you left. As we pulled into our bay for the evening, a dead snake lay on the little gravel road, it did not fill me with much confidence. If Bear Grylls had been there, he would have been out eating scorpions and drinking his own pee. By contrast to those wild survivor type people, we sat and ate 'M and Ms' whilst drinking Yorkshire tea - real adventurers.

Chapter 24

A Meteor, Flagstaff and the Grand Canyon

Waking at an RV site in Arizona is unlike most things you will ever do in your life. If you have not done it and you are thinking about where to go and what to see in America, just spend one day watching the sunset and rise over Arizona, a more majestic and beautiful thing you will struggle to find.

The days in Arizona are baking hot, the sun relentless in its effort to cook you. The nights contrastingly leave you scrambling for more layers while the beads of sweat that had been rolling down your face turn to ice. Arizona is a desert.

I had managed pain well throughout the entire trip. Painkillers were taken when needed and anti-inflammatories were choked down like Skittles. On the route from Winslow to Flagstaff, my right knee burnt, not like a carpet burn, it burnt like it was being heated from the inside out, like somehow my knee was in a microwave. I managed 20 miles with the pain.

There were no rest days at all planned across the entire route; the reason for this was that we didn't have many days spare. I am teacher, first and foremost, and I needed to be back by the start of September for the new term and I also had a rather pressing engagement in Las Vegas. I was getting married a few days after the run was scheduled to be completed. I had given myself a few days of a buffer in case the worst happened and I was not able to keep moving at all. After 20 miles my knee would take no more, I still had 30 miles to complete that day but there was no way that running was an option.

The bike was always there as my plan B, if I couldn't run anymore. It was according to most a slightly easier way to get the mileage in. Granted, the bike would eat up the miles quicker than running, the problem was, though, that I had spent the previous day on the bike and my body needed the rest. However, there was no other option - it was the bike or stop and I didn't want to stop.

I pressed as hard and as fast as I could towards Flagstaff, this would be where we would rest for the evening. The ride was spectacular, the combination of scenery and serenity combined was breath-taking.

As we moved along the highway we saw signs for a 'Meteor Crater', the team and I decided it was worth a visit and I quickly blasted out the last few miles on the bike. One advantage of doing such a short stint on the bike was that the day was over quite quickly and this meant that my body had a little bit more time to recover.

The Meteor Crater was about 10 miles off the highway, it is sign-posted and it is quite a large tourist attraction, if you are ever in the area. There is little I can say about it to be honest, it's exactly what it says on the tin, a Meteor Crater. It's not some little dip in the ground, though, this is massive on a whole new scale.

It takes telescopes and binoculars to see across it and there are sight-seeing walks around it. Standing there on the edge of the crater gave me a great sense of how small we are and how something from outer space could cause absolute devastation, if it collided with a city or town.

Meteor Crater.

On the way to the RV site in Flagstaff I had seen a sign stating that we were 80 miles from the Grand Canyon. I sat quietly for ages, going about my little jobs on the RV, watching people mill around the site. As evening fell and we settled down for something to eat, I asked the team a question. "Guys....." I said in a tone which implied that there was more to come, "it is pointless coming all this way, to America, to Arizona, and not seeing the Grand Canyon." I was hoping that they would all feel the same way. I told them of the sign I had seen on the drive in and I also told them that if I was on the bike and going well I could knock 80 miles off in a few hours, meaning that day would not be much longer than normal. The answer from the ream was a resounding, "HELL YES!" So it was settled, at 5am the following morning we would head out of Flagstaff and north towards the Grand Canyon.

Plans and maps were stared at throughout the evening, tough areas were pointed out and long sections highlighted on the map. I spoke to the RV site owner; he was a brilliant guide for the area, pointing out where good viewing areas were and where we would be able to park the RV. He told me about the 1,000 foot climb heading out of Flagstaff that might cause me some problems but also that after this it was the most scenic and stunning ride I could possibly imagine - he was not wrong.

Arizona had moved us into another time zone, so we were now 8 hours behind the UK. It was 5am in Flagstaff when we departed the RV site, excitement and anticipation filled the air. I tucked in behind the RV and hit my straps early, we were off. As I cycled towards the outskirts of the town I looked to my right as a deer ran parallel to me, gracefully and camply prancing its way through the field, barely touching the ground. It parted company with me after half a mile and disappeared into the woods that surrounded Arizona.

I continued out of the town and began the ascent, it was going to take me from the 7,000 feet we had got to in Flagstaff up to 8,000 feet at the top. It sounds hard and awful, and to tell you it wasn't would be a lie. I slogged my way up the hill, feeling like at any point snails would come zooming past me. I reached the summit, breathing heavy, almost wheezing, but I did it.

As my wheels ticked over the top I saw a sign. This was a sign that was foreign to me so far on this trip. 'Downhill' the sign read, '6% decline, check your brakes', I did no such thing, I was off. I was a blur of white and ginger as I shot down the slope, my speedometer almost breaking on the way down.

Since arriving home and talking to people about my adventures, I am often asked what the best bit was or which bit I would like to do again. When I answer I always say that descent. If ever you get the chance to go to America and cycle, choose the route from Flagstaff to Cameron, heading North on the 89. I assure you this is the most fun you will have ever have on a bike, whether you like cycling or not.

As we arrived at the south rim of the Canyon, we parked up the RV and I decided to get changed. I thought it best not to visit one of the world's most amazing natural attractions with my sponge sticking out – I thought it would probably tarnish the memory a tad.

The name 'Grand Canyon' does not do it justice at all, I mean "Grand" is all well and good but this thing is something else. It makes anything you have ever looked at and thought was amazing seem mundane and quite simply average. Any other canyon should just be called 'Not Even Close Canyon'. I felt like I needed more sets of eyes to take it all in, even now I don't think I appreciated quite what I was looking at, it was..... well, it was just - WOW.

I can only implore you to go there now. Go, go now. Pack your bag and get out of the door and go. If you are bothered about money, save every penny you can and then go, take anyone and everyone you can with you and make sure they see it, there is nothing there that can disappoint you. If you want to see the best of it, go early, we arrived at about 8am, and there was hardly a car in the car park. There are not the words to do it justice, it really is incredible.

Grand Canyon.

Coming away from the Grand Canyon the entire team was on a high. It was a brilliant start to the morning as we moved south again and back towards our original route. I was riding fast and strong, a new wave of adrenaline and hope rushed through my body, the smile could not be taken from my face. Pedalling and singing as I went, it was Epic. We passed an abundance of wildlife on the way including deer, elk, mountain lions and coyotes. Arizona just kept on giving. We pummelled our way down from the Grand Canyon. My legs were pumping furiously as I maintained the pace, often pushing from 35 to 40 miles per hour as we continued down towards our rest area of Kingman.

As I reached Kingman that evening I was once again empty, although the day had been exhilarating and exciting, the heat, altitude and pain had still been constant. You would be forgiven, whilst reading this, for thinking that I find pain pleasant or that some days were easy and they just passed by without ache or incident. This is simply not true - in fact, it could not be further from the truth. The truth is that every day hurt – a lot. Not like a little graze or cut which hurts for a second, this was bone-crunching, joint-pounding agony. On the way up to the Grand Canyon I had removed another toe nail, the pliers had come out and once again a toe nail was the victim. If you have not a pulled a toe nail out of your own body before, don't try it, it is excruciating.

I listen to people now, at work or in the gym talking about the pain they are in from a run or ride they have just done and I often wonder what their concept of pain is, what are they comparing it to? Pain is what you make of it, if you say the pain is 10 out of 10, then your mind will tell you that it is really bad, it is unbearable. With me I try and compare my current pain to pain that I have experienced before. I am almost always able to remember a time when I have felt worse and when I am able to do this, my current pain doesn't seem that bad. I am sure this isn't what other people do and this probably wouldn't be recommended by experts, but it works for me.

Chapter 25

The Last State, Wild Donkeys?

Arizona had given me everything it could, climb after climb had come at me, ferocious heat had attacked me on a daily basis but as it tried to beat me to my knees it had also given me hope. What I had seen and experienced in Arizona could not be eclipsed by any negatives. As such, to Arizona all I can do now is say thank you.

I pressed out of Kingman in the early hours, joined once again by Kerry who stuck with me through my first 10 kilometres. It was a wet and dreary run, with drizzle hanging heavily over us as we tracked our way along the 66, parallel to the interstate. We plodded along still a little buoyed by the experiences of the previous day, a slight spring in our step during our slow run. The weather did what it could to dampen our spirits, as we passed over the interstate towards Oatman, the rain intensified.

Before arriving at the 'Ghost Town' Oatman, we had the slight issue of a range of mountains. I had been watching the mountains all morning as the road swung and snaked towards them, knowing that at some point I would be heading over them. Off in the distance about half way up the first mountain the road disappeared, it then reappeared much further up on the second mountain.

So far that morning I had run with all except one member of the team. Kerry, Helen and Saj had all joined me at some point on the road. We had all sweated and plodded together. However, as the climbing really began, Darren was the unlucky support act. Darren joined me and we fell into perfect military timing, each foot landing at the same time. The sound of each foot hitting in unison became something to focus on, helping us to ignore the huge obstacle in front of us. We continued unerringly up the hill. We joked that maybe like some of the hills on the journey previously it might be merely an optical illusion and that when we got there it would in fact be quite flat, our jokes and smiles were short lived.

The ascent that had started off gradually but it had become steeper than any climb so far, contouring round the mountain, the bends continuing for miles into the distance, doubling back on themselves so that it wasn't too steep for vehicles. "Never quit on a hill!" I screamed at myself, sweat flowing off my head as slugged my way up, step by step towards the summit. After 6 miles of climbing Darren had hit his limit, he had done his job, he had got me this far. As Darren found some sanctuary in the RV and got his breath back, Helen and Saj joined me again. This time we were going all the way to the top.

I love to see the look on people's faces as they pass me while I run, especially somewhere as remote as mountains. On this occasion, we were miles from anywhere, we had been running for 30 miles already and we were not quite at the top. Yet, as they passed and tooted their horns, even cheered sometimes, I smiled, I wanted them to know that I could do this, that this climb would not beat me. As I hit the top, and like many times during this adventure I was hit with an overwhelming sense of euphoria. I had done it - not just I - we had done it, we had conquered that mountain.

We descended into Oatman shortly after lunch time. Oatman is described in tourist leaflets as a 'Ghost Town', so we were a little surprised to see a town full of hustle and bustle and even more surprised to see, wild donkeys. We had seen so many abandoned towns along the way that this seemed quite odd to have the title of 'Ghost Town' when it was by far busier than the rest of the towns put together. Perhaps some of the other towns should be selling themselves in the same way and maybe then they would have thriving businesses. As for the donkeys, well, these by all accounts had been released into the wild when the town was emptied after the gold rush. They took to the land and have been living wild ever since. They walk up and down the road like any person would, completely oblivious to what's going on around them.

Having done the touristy thing, and taken a few pictures, we pressed out of Oatman and towards California. Our rest area for the night was in a town called Needles. We passed the state line by going over a bridge that evening, right in the middle of the water we went from Arizona to California. It was obvious we were in California too, the landscape and the trees changed within just a few feet of the state line. Palm trees now lined the sides of the streets, slightly angled in to make it look like they were hugging the roads. The smell, the mountains and even the grass are just slightly different in California, it seems more relaxed, more laid back than the places we had been to previously. I was nearly there now, no more state lines to cross.

Chapter 26

The Desert, but almost Home

The desert is a strange place. It's dry (obviously) but with an almost a serene beauty that I had not expected. White plains of sand, stretch miles and miles into the distance, it is lifeless for the most part with the odd sprinkling of greenery.

I pedalled behind the RV, drafting as we had done over the previous week in order to maintain pace but also to protect myself a little bit. Behind the back of the RV, when in the desert, was a horrendous place to be, it was a cauldron of hot air and dust. I describe it as like cycling inside a vacuum cleaner bag that is above a fire, as you heave in hot air, your lungs feel flooded and strangely warm.

As the heat of the day broke through, I began to slowly roast, like a turkey at Christmas I was starting to cook. The temperature pushed to 39 degrees and with that a drinks break was in order. There was no escaping the heat; I went from a sweaty vacuum bag behind the RV to microwave conditions in the RV.

We made a plan to try and break the day down into one hour blocks, knowing that if I could keep my average pace up towards 25 miles per hour I would be done in 8 hours with rests and drink stops. I was carrying my water on the bike so that I didn't have to stop every time I needed a drink, the only problem with that was the fact that my water began to get warm very quickly. There is very little that is less refreshing than abnormally warm drinking water. I can now see why the professional cyclists are so small, it's nothing to do with power to weight ratios, it's the fact that when the sun is out your back acts like a giant solar panel. I was soaking up heat extremely quickly and I couldn't cool down. The air conditioning unit on the RV was as much use as a chocolate teapot. My saving grace arrived in the shape of an outpost shop, the air conditioning in there was nearly enough to make me sleep there for the night.

Day 30 was my last full day on the bike, the last 150 miles I would cover on Tallulah. She had done so well. She might not be perfect, she might change gear sometimes just when she feels like it but she had got me to a point where I was almost finished.

We spent our penultimate evening at an RV site in a place called Victorville, it was a great little RV site where we could watch wildlife and life drift by. I sat and watched some rabbits and squirrels playing around a tree, like a scene out of Bambi they somehow seemed to know each other. At this point, I thought back to my first day in New York, one month earlier - the rain and streets seemed like a life time ago, I could not believe how far we had come.

Day 31 was my last full day of running. We pushed out of Victorville early, passing some of the more interesting inhabitants. One man was carrying a freezer on the front of his bike and a few others were definitely only just coming in after a night out. It was developing into a nice day, the sun coming up over the mountains lit up the little town. Sign-posts and advertising boards pointed the way to LA.

We began our descent towards LA by dropping into the suburbs of Fontana and Pomona. We found ourselves on leafy little streets, with a relaxed what might be described as 'Californian' feel. As I looked out towards downtown LA, the smog sat heavily over the city, it was a warning of what was to come but it also showed me how close we were. The roads were wide and quiet, cars shuffled by at a relaxed pace. There was no rushing or screaming on the streets in this area, I was reminded of a retirement village.

We pulled into the RV site in Pomona, our last night on the RV. My last night in that tiny sweaty bed, but weirdly I would miss it, I knew already that I would miss it. I still missed the campervan from the original 'Epic run'. I would miss waking up every day somewhere different. The RV site was just what we needed for our last night; a chance to sit and relax, to plan our strategy for the city and to picture finishing what we had started one month previously - we were almost there.

Chapter 27

The finish

To say I was emotional was an understatement of monumental proportions, I don't even think there is a word to describe how I felt. I could barely sit on the bike that morning I was sick with excitement, but ultimately I was ready to finish.

I had lost two stone in weight, I had lost most of my toe nails and I had sweated an immeasurable number of litres but on Day 32, I finished my 'Epic Adventure'. Under my own steam, I had made it across a continent. I had run 50 miles one day followed by cycling 150 miles the next across America, with my fantastic team behind me and a smile on my face (most of the time), I had done it.

I remember laying on my hotel bed that evening and I could stretch my legs out right to the bottom. I could go to the toilet without banging my head or waking up 4 other people. I could feel the air conditioning unit cooling my skin but most of all I could lay there knowing that the next day I didn't have run or cycle anywhere.

As cycling days go it wasn't actually great, we pushed out of Pomona and there we were met with rush hour traffic - a concept that had become somewhat foreign to us over the last few weeks. It was stop, start, junction to junction, never really moving at all. The team shuffled through maps searching for 'Bike routes in LA'. They were trying frantically to find me a better way to Santa Monica Pier.

I made a few turns, the radio in my pocket barking orders at me. As I moved through the streets we hit a slip lane and were heading towards a Freeway and 8 lanes of LA rush hour traffic. I dismounted quickly and jumped on the RV. I would run the remaining 20 miles down to the pier, Darren would be by my side on the bike to make sure I was safe and carry my water. The rest of the team would meet us on the pier, at the finish line.

As I ran, Darren tootled along on the bike next to me, we buzzed along the LA streets, necessarily avoiding the majority of the locals in the downtown area. The sights and smells of LA were mesmeric. The concrete jungle of buildings was eye-catching and somehow different from anything I had ever seen before.

We pulled over for a drink, hitting what can only be described as the more affluent area of LA. "Single digits, Sam," Darren said with a little smile. "Single sodding digits!" I replied. We both then fell silent, thinking about the journey and how far we had come. 3,000 miles and we were down to single digits, we were almost there.

Off we went again, heading for Colorado Avenue and onto Santa Monica Pier for the finish. Darren pushed on ahead, he would meet the rest of the team on the pier and allow me to finish by myself, with my run onto the pier.

If you were there while I ran through those streets in LA, I can only apologise. I couldn't speak and emotion had taken hold of me. Tears streamed down my face as I ran, I powered down the street towards the ocean, buildings, people and street names were and are still a blur to me. I was almost there.

I ran up the small foot bridge that connects to the pier but people were moving painfully slow on the pavement. I jumped the chain and sprinted towards the pier, as I moved I could hear the shouts and screams, I could see the team and the finish line, I was almost there.

As I hit the finish line I didn't know what I should feel, an overwhelming surge of emotion hit me, I had done it, and I was there. As I embraced Kerry, I knew I had completed the toughest challenge of my life, America had thrown everything it had at me, but I had survived.

It's a strange feeling to have completed something that took over your life for so long, to have done the impossible, to win. We had done it; The 'Epic Adventure' Team had made it across America. We are not a team of doctors, we are not sponsored athletes or even sponsored anything, we are team of friends, and we had done it.

To anyone out there who is dreaming of an adventure I say this to you - GO. Go and be amazing, listen to the 8 year old inside you, climb the mountains, ride the bike and run up and down the hills, and whilst you do it, most importantly of all, SMILE.

So for me, I bid you good night.

America, thank you for the memories.

Sam Boatwright

(STILL SMILING)

At the finish line, Santa Monica Pier.

My Blog

This is my raw unedited Facebook blog from my Epic Adventure. There is no spelling corrections or grammatical changes, it is taken word for word as it was done on the journey. I hope it gives you a small insight into my everyday life on the road.

Day 1.

The end of a long and punishing day. Absolutely shattered. Feet are in tatters. I had tried to ease myself in. Turned into a 15 hour day. Still not quite finished. For those that are wondering about my feet, I think the toenails will be gone in the next few days. Thanks for all the support. At each rest stop I look at all the messages, the likes and the shares. Tomorrow sees us head to Washington. It will be another long day but this time will be all day in the saddle. Tomorrow is another day. #theadventurecontinues

Day 2.

So, apparently you can't cycle down the highway. Policeman said "you can't ride down the highway man, you'll get yourself killed." Hitting the smaller roads now! Pressing great this morning! Feel much better. Legs feel good.

Day 2 finished. I've pushed as hard and as fast as I can today. We made some great time this morning until the police caught up with us. Cycling on the smaller roads is ok but much tougher climbs! Had a big blow out this afternoon with my rear tyre, which when pushing at 40mph is not a pleasant experience! Managed to change the tyre and get moving again. Very stop/start with traffic. We have had to drive to the RV site tonight so we will drive back into Washington early tomorrow and run past the White House. These have been two very long hard days. First ice bath tonight in the paddling pool! Currently have the ice packs just on my knees. Well done everyone on the likes! I think your goal should be 5000 by the time I hit LA! Apologies to those people who are being bombarded with shared posts and invitations to like the page!

Second day of running tomorrow, hopefully the weather is better! #beepic #run #cycle #america

Day 3.

Not a bad day at all. The weather we faced in New York has changed very quickly. Unbelievably warm today. Sweat just poured out from the first steps. Have taken the advice of friends and wrapped my toes up. They do feel a bit better but not going to try and take the tape off as I think the nails will come with it. We are staying in a rest area tonight, which I'm hoping is better than last night as we had 4000000 bugs in the RV last night as we stayed near what we thought had to be a jungle! Not much sleep was had! A lot of screaming was done. Enjoyed the miles today. Back on the bike tomorrow. Hurt my elbow today when a car wing mirror hit me!

Day 4.

Not the start I wanted. My seat stem broke, so I couldn't ride my bike first thing. Instead, ran 13 miles to the nearest town or place that at least had a shop and went to a garage who luckily had a spare screw! Once on the bike was able to get some good mileage in until we hit the mountains. Today's steepest climb was a 2915 ft climb which doesn't sound too bad but when you do that 7 times it gets slightly tiring. We have made the mileage but it was a long hard slog. Was some of the toughest miles I've ever spent in the saddle. Without the team today I would have failed. Had good support from local people today which is great, so much needed at the moment. One person wrote to me saying the mountains I was cycling up were hard even in a car!

The ice bath was a little different tonight. Stopped next to a river and decided rather than the paddling pool again I would just lay in the water! Was beautiful! Weather has been hot and humid again today, suppose to break tomorrow with thunder storms. New York seems like a distant memory now. Heading to Pittsburg tomorrow. 2 of the team leave tomorrow and I'm absolutely gutted they are going. They have been fantastic and I will be forever in their debt for what they have given up to be here. Thank you. To everyone who has shared and liked the page you are brilliant. Please keep those likes coming, they make me smile every time. All social media handles are twitter @samboatwright1 Instagram @epicrunningsam and the website is samboat wright.com. #smile #epic #thanksguys

Day 5.

Another warm one today. Today restored my faith in humanity, my faith in the power of Facebook and just exactly why I wanted to do this. Tonight we sit with Peg and John, at their beautiful home in Pittsburg. The local people have been brilliant today, bringing out Gatorade, water and even donating to Helpforheroes charity. Thank you to everyone! I love waking up to all the likes and comments it's brilliant! What was brilliant was looking at how many people the posts have reached - 35,000 people! That's incredible. Thank you to every single one of you.

Kerry and helen both ran with me today. Kerry did 20 miles this morning - a great effort. I think she now appreciates how much pain your legs can truly be in! The best shout out attempt so far has to be Dan Higgins who has written to Arnold Schwarzenegger!! Loved that. Tomorrow we head to Colombus on the bike. Today has been a good day. I never expected this heat! I am starting to think that Forest Gump was not based on real life events! As I'm sure during that film he does not say "ow my f**king legs!" Legs are numbing off quicker in a morning now so I can get into a rhythm quite fast. Already looking forward to what tomorrow will bring but for now. It's time to eat and snooze! #beepic #America #faith #people

Day 6.

I hurt. Everything hurts. My hands hurt from holding the handle bars, legs are in bits, neck, back, shoulders and feet just hurt. Didn't get much sleep last night, there was flash floods in Pittsburg and when the rain hit the RV it sounded like we were being invaded. We pressed hard out of Pittsburg this morning clocking up great mileage in torrential rain. Had my full Weezle kit on today. For any cyclists out there, scuba gear is fantastic on wet rides as it dries mega quick and keeps you warm. Went through loads of little towns today, all exactly how you imagine America to be. White picket fences, kids playing baseball, people sitting on their front porches..... and then a big sweaty Yorkshireman huffing and puffing his way across America comes storming past. After a quick bite to eat at dinner I was able to lose some of the layers as the sun came out. We pressed along towards Columbus. We are sat on the outskirts of Columbus. 11 and a half hours in the saddle today. With breaks and stops makes this a 13 hour day. The rain of this morning seems so long ago. I just need sleep. I run tomorrow which my ass will be very happy with but my feet will be screaming at. Thanks again for all the support. I've been told my tracker isn't working at the moment. Hopefully will be back up and running soon. I'm often asked why I do this...... I would love to come up with something profound and inspiring right now, but I don't have the energy. I run for those that can't. Simple. Sam

Day 7.

A good day running. 28 degrees in Ohio today but without the humidity of the last few days. Ran well this morning, punched out my first marathon in 4.17 which I was pretty happy with. This afternoon was a little tougher as the sun started to bake me. I've added some pics from the bike yesterday and some from today. I have a lot of pics of me on the bike and they all look like I am on the same road. They are actually different roads! I met a guy today called Burt Montgomery, a 90 year old army vet who served in Korea. He was out on his lawnmower mowing the grass on the side of his 2000 acre soya bean farm. He donated 20 dollars. What a great guy. I also saw two people going to the supermarket on sit on lawn mowers! They did their full weekly shop and then drove off bags and all! Today I hit 12,000 calories burnt for the day. Tonight we are in Loveland Ohio. We are staying with a friend from university. A beautiful place. Thanks for all the messages. I can't tell you enough how much I appreciate them! They are what keep me going. We have debated today about what I could call my next book about this challenge. Any ideas? Let's see what you guys can come up with. Tomorrow we are on the bike again. 150 miles here we come!

Day 8.

Batesville. After a great night with friends we got out on the bike in good time. Today has been a shorter day. We have worked hard over the last few to take today down to 81 miles. I needed and the team needed it too. We are currently sat at an RV site taking in some sun and trying to use a couple of hours extra to recover. Tomorrow I run to Indianapolis and then onto Chicago. I can't thank Sion and Shelly enough for their hospitality last night. I don't think they quite know how much it meant to the whole team. The cycling today was hard even though it was only 81 miles. The Tarmac wasn't quite as smooth with a lot of potholes which made me feel like I was working much harder than normal. We have taken some time to restock the RV. We know the next push is going to be very hard. The heat has changed from hot and humid to a more dry heat. The heat is the one thing I was fearsome of and it is proving very very hard going. I can feel my body losing shape. It almost feels like it's turning soft?! It's 30 degrees here today and only going to get hotter as we cross Route 66. Sun cream, Gatorade and H20. Thank you for all the donations! We are nearly at £1000. The likes on FB are getting close to 5000. I reckon with one big push we could make it to the 5000! Come on Facebook let's see what you've got! #getto5000 #likes #helpforheroes #epic #adventure

Day 9.

A long day of running. Was warm again but thankfully not as warm as yesterday. Thunderstorms were forecast but we just hand the thunder and no rain. I could have done with some rain. Just needed to cool down. Had two cold showers when I came in for a drink just to try and stop sweating, they seem to be helping. We are in greenfield tonight outside of Indianapolis in the state of Indiana. Everyone has run with me today at some point. It took a long time for my legs to free up this morning and allow me to get into my stride. Once moving I felt ok but there was a dull ache all day through my left quad. Thank you for the donations overnight and throughout the day. We have just moved over £1000. It was amazing to have John Bishop share my page last night. It might not mean much to him, one quick share, but it makes a massive difference to me so thank you

John. Tomorrow we head towards Chicago. We will be at the start of Route 66! Might be a little late starting tomorrow as the RV lost a wing mirror today when we hit another car! This needs to be fixed before we set off. I love that my little brother was on the radio this morning talking about the run! I'll be on BFBS Radio tomorrow morning before we depart. All in all a good day. Hard running and hot running but the miles did tick by over the 11 hours.

Day 10.

Double figures, quite pleasing to get to double figures. Was a painful day. When I'm on the bike it's not my legs that's the problem but my ass! It's the time spent in the saddle. This morning for the first two hours I averaged 22.5mph which is pretty good. This was while the sun was still coming up and the heat of the day was still weak. The cycling through Indiana was not hard, like the mountains earlier in the challenge. It's just long straight and flat, very very flat. The roads stretch until they haze with the heat. I imagine if it was just for a day it would seem quite pleasant. Corn fields as far as the eye can see. The towns are ones like Bruce Springsteen would sing about. All of them with a sign saying "go panthers" or "go vikings" whichever their high school team might be. We stopped to rest in Frankfort today. A beautiful town, like all of them with a big water tower as you enter with the name of the town on the side.

I did a radio interview this morning which was quite fun. I never know what to say when people ask me, why?

Today we are in Chicago and once again thanks to Sion and Shelley we are staying in a hotel. A bed, the things we take for granted. Tomorrow we start on Route 66. It's going to be 28 degrees tomorrow. At least I feel like we are moving west now and towards LA. This picture has made me laugh a lot. I'm feeling a lot of support from home. Thank you. Each day we chat about how many people have seen the post and the comments people have made. Let's hope tomorrow is a good day. #epic #beinspired #run #cycle

Day 11.

Started the proper Route 66 this morning, although if I'm honest it was a bit of anti climax. Chicago is a brilliant vibrant city, with great people and fantastic buildings. The only sign post that lets you know you're on Route 66 is the one in the picture. The real Route 66 and the historic road doesn't really start Gardner. We stopped in Gardner for something to eat. The running out of Chicago was pretty good, good through all the different boroughs and through Chinatown. Once in the historic road this afternoon you seem to go back in time. The towns have old fuel pumps and really make an effort to get the old fashioned feel of Route 66. Was pushing a good pace this morning running 8 minute miles, this slowed to 10 minute miles later this afternoon and I was still running as the sun went down. Today I got some very special donations. I don't normally do shout outs but I wanted to say a huge thank you to Matthew, Tom and Lucy. They donated their pocket money. It nearly broke me more than the run to know you did that. We are camped up now. I can already hear the crickets!

150 miles on the bike tomorrow. Into a head wind.

Almost a stone down in weight now. The majority of that was sweated out in the humid heat of Chicago this morning. My aim I now think is to do this, inspire the uninspired. Tonight I'll leave you with a quote. "Train hard under the dark lights, to shine under the bright lights".

Day 12.

This day should just read "head wind". What a killer of a day this has been. Constantly pressing into a head wind was hard work. Have to push so much harder to maintain an average speed. The crew were shattered today. Last night was freezing cold for some reason. I'm always warm so it didn't bother me much the guys suffered. I wore full tights and long sleeved top to cycle in. Today we rest in Springfield. Home of Abraham Lincoln and of course The Simpsons. Haven't got quite as far as I had hoped today but it was either a very long day to a rest area or rest a little earlier and have a nice camp site. Tomorrow we will push out running towards St. Louis. I'm hoping the wind drops a little. The problem with long straight roads is that once the wind is against you, it's against you for the next 20 miles straight. Over the last two days I have listened to music for the first time since being in the US. Playlist included

- linkin park - hybrid theory
- Bruce Springsteen - Born in the USA
  And just to camp things up a little bit.
- Joseph and the amazing technicolored dreamcoat.

Yes, each one of these songs was sung at the top of my voice. America has not seen many 6'3, 15 stone tattooed fellas singing show tunes at the top of their lungs. The locals got a real treat.

The main aim of today was to get Saj to sing the carpenters while we looked for the campsite. He wouldn't sing it, even though I know he knew all the words!

Everyday we wake up and check the comments people have made. We check the donations from over night. Thank you for your continued support. Tomorrow we will run. I made some adaptations today to my padded shorts and stuffed a sponge down the back of them. Seemed to work pretty well. It's fine until I stop to talk to someone and it looks like I literally "sh*t a brick". It's not a good look at all but helped me stay on the bike a few hours more. We are still edging closer to the 5000 likes. I think one big push could be close??? #get5000 #5000likes #inspire #bike #run #150 #50

Day 13.

I'm struggling to think of ways to describe long straight roads.... so today there were once again, long straight roads. You would be forgiven in thinking you had gone in a circle, many of the roads look like another. Miles and miles of corn fields with roads dissecting then into perfect squares. The pictures show a few different things. One is my hat from today when I rested at lunch. The marks on it is the salt drying from my sweat. It was a good day running today. I am able to push quite well in the morning and generally getting about 30 miles in and then resting for lunch leaving me with a smaller couple of runs in the afternoon. I'm finding the running easier than the cycling, I couldn't tell you why. I dread each day getting on the bike. Run days are about 10 or

11 hours. Bike days have been 12-15 hours. For those tracking us we are about 1 day behind schedule. I wanted to try and get abit of the mileage back today but I was too tired. Yesterday beat me til I had nothing left. I was empty at the start of today from the wind yesterday. Hopefully somewhere I can catch up. Nothing over 20 miles is enjoyable, every step drags and the noise of your trainers hitting Tarmac starts to send you slowly insane. The miles from 20-50 are lonely boring miles. Every member of the team ran with me at some point today, it's great when they do that. Even not talking but having someone there just makes each step a little easier. One of the pics I have posted is from the bike yesterday, it shows the magic sponge. Don't knock it til you have tried it! The other picture is a sign we passed today. 1907 miles to LA. It should just say "a long chuffing way Boatwright!". I was joined on my run today by Kimee Armour. Kimee is a para athlete who is competing at the para games in two weeks. She is competing in the Duathlon. She saw me running this morning so went home and came out for a training run with me. It was brilliant. We are just outside St. Louis this evening. A few people have asked what I'm eating.... well, it depends, but generally I'm eating as much as I can. Breakfast is fruit salad with yogurt and granola. Mid morning maybe a coffee and protein bar. Lunch is a turkey wrap or chicken sandwich. Afternoon I'll grab anything with calories....doughnut/cake/chocolate. Evening meals have been salads, chilli or spaghetti bolognese. That's a pretty normal day. Alongside this is a lot of water and Gatorade! Another question I was asked is where people can see my progress. Just use the live tracker on samboatwright.com that's the best way.

Back on the bike tomorrow with my new best friend "the sponge". Keep doing what you're doing your end and I'll keep moving this end. Sam.

Day 14.

We have been on the road for 2 weeks now. New York seems like a distant memory. Passed through St.Louis this morning, it's home to the Gateway Arch, apparently the largest free standing arch in the world. Was great to be there early in the morning, the streets were empty. I loved the look and feel of St. Louis, much more than I have some of the other cities we have passed. It was clean and had a great vibrancy about it. After St. Louis we stuck to the historic Route 66 as much as we could. Helen was navigating this morning and thought it would be good to forget which her left and right was, first thing, wrong turn up a huge climb. I'm glad it was first thing and not last thing. Once we found the right road it was great riding, the magic sponge doing its job and the miles flew by. Anyone who loves cycling would have enjoyed the ride this morning, smooth tarmac, no traffic and almost no hills. The historic route runs parallel with the interstate which sometimes ruins the serenity of the ride. Big rolling wagons thundering along the road at one side with fields and forests at the other. Today was the first time we saw how much the interstate has devastated the local towns and businesses, so many houses left derelict and so many business with "closed down" signs on them. Interspersed between the closed down shops and abandoned houses are the real gems of America. The worlds largest rocking chair, the town of bourbon and the town of Cuba. Cuba was brilliant, I didn't see one chain store just all family stores and local business. The bike was ok today. Mechanically it's not going great, much like my body it's creaking a bit with the constant pounding of the road. My bike is called Talula much to the amusement of the team. It's the same name given to the Jamaican Bobsleigh teams bobsleigh in Cool Runnings. Like their bobsleigh, it's nothing too fancy, it was bought off eBay 5 years ago but I trust that she will do the job. This post comes to you from a truck park. I can hear the traffic from the interstate, it's not glamorous, far from it in fact but to me it's perfect. It's everything adventure should be. #inspire #smilebig

Day 15.

I'm sure today will be one of those days where I look back in the days, weeks, months and years to come and think to myself "that was really stupid". Today was a 100k day or 62.5 miles (ish) Everything hurts. I have managed to get back 12.5 miles of the 50 miles we were behind. It was some of the toughest running I have ever done.

We got away to a great start. Having spent the night at a truck stop in Doolittle where due to the heat I got about 4.5 seconds of sleep. Today was the day where going down hill gets worse than going up. Going up effects my heart and lungs, makes me work a bit harder, I can cope with that. Going downhill feels like someone is ramming red hot pokers through my knees and up into my quads. I broke the day into 4 sections, trying to do 25k at a time. It worked, to a point. Over the trip so far I have lost 1 stone in weight. Today, I lost 11lb in one day. Just the third 25k cost me 5lb in weight. The team were panicking so much they were googling whether it's healthy to sweat so much. I am staying hydrated but I almost can't keep up with the amount that's coming out. Although horrible I am happy with the day. There were some great sites. One place called Uranus. They have a fudge company. Fudge made in Uranus. All of the shops and business were funny uses of the word Uranus. The best was the sign as you left which said "Thanks for picking Uranus". As I ran this morning I hear a scream from Helen as she screams look at the sign Sam. The sign read "Tan your fanny", brilliant. Without the team today I can safely say I wouldn't have made the 100k. I got back on the RV and was shaking, dizzy and was on the edge of passing out. Kerry literally had to feed me. Stuffing tablets in my throats and pouring water in my mouth and an ice pack on my head. I could tell I was suffering when even my watch felt heavy on my wrist.

We passed a town this morning called Devils Elbow. I'll never forget that climb. It went on forever. Tonight we are staying just outside Springfield. This is the second Springfield we have stopped in. This may well be my last post. The RV site we are at I'm pretty sure could be the setting for any scary movie ever! I was amazed when I went for a shower that 1. I came out alive and 2. I don't appear to have contracted any diseases, but it's $25 dollars a night and they have running water. We can't complain.

Tomorrow I'm on the bike again, heading out early to Joplin. What today has done to my body won't really be seen or felt till tomorrow. There was a tornado in Tulsa, Oklahoma today. We are moving that way over the next few days..... (don't worry mum, I can run fast when I need too). Thanks again for all the support, I know I say it nearly everyday but it means everything. #100club #pain #heals #run

Day 16.

It's a warm one today. We survived the night, which was a huge bonus. Actually slept pretty well. My nipples after yesterday have worn down to nothingness!

As always we have stayed away from the main highways choosing the smaller country roads. Our RV is 12 feet tall, the bridge was 10 feet tall. Sometimes it's impossible for us to stick to the historic Route 66 so we have to navigate our way through the little towns and tiny roads till we meet the 66 again. I pedalled for an hour this morning before I even saw one car. At times I like the peace and quiet but the bike is already a lonely place, too much peace, soon becomes difficult. We passed through Mount Vernon this morning, one of the larger towns today. I always check the populations as I pass. Some of the larger towns might have 50,000 where others are 150!

The houses seem so isolated, I often wonder who lives there? Do they have a family? How do they see people? Where do they do their big shop at?

I hadn't really noticed or felt the weight loss until today, clothes are not fitting quite the same. For me I've noticed it the most on my arms and chest. My arms look like pieces of string with a knot in the middle for my elbow.

I had the opportunity to put more miles in today and get back on track but yesterday has emptied me. I couldn't face another hill. The hills in Missouri are massively different to home. They are not huge but just enough that I have to push a little harder and lose my momentum. Some do drag and at that point the sweat pours like someone has turned on a tap. Talula creaked and groaned her way over the line today. She took some real hammer on one decent. The terrain was like the Paris Roubaix, by the bottom of the decent my fingers, wrist and elbows were in pieces.

As I came to a finish today eagles circled over my head. I had watched earlier in the day ahead of me in the road as three eagles shredded an armadillo roadkill. It made me nervous thinking they were circling, waiting for me to drop!

Tonight we are just outside Joplin. We are on the state lines between Missouri, Kansas and Oklahoma. Tomorrow I'll run into Oklahoma. As we move west the temperatures continue to increase. Let's see what tomorrow brings. #beepic #run #cycle #inspire

Day 17.

Any day I have ever moaned about, any time I have ever felt pain, been too hot or too cold pales into insignificance after today. The heat today has been unbelievable. I know it only topped out at 32 degrees but there was just no hiding from the sun. The long stretches of road, haze in the distance as the heat comes off the road. Normally I breeze a six mile run. It's a pleasant run that would take 50 minutes, maybe an hour if it was casual. Today took me 1 hour and 40 minutes to run the last 6 miles. I collapsed into Kerrys arms as I finished. I don't remember finishing today, I remember feeling dizzy and stumbling. As I sat on the RV I just went cold, my legs like jelly, the team got me through.

I would love to tell you how amazing the scenery was today, but it was dull. Long stretches of road, I begged for a hill, a corner, a bridge, flipping anything but straight roads! It was like running a 10k race but you're the only competitor and it's just a straight line to the finish, but you can't see the finish line as it's too flipping hot!

As we left Joplin this morning, we crossed the state line into Oklahoma near Seneca. Passing through Wyandotte and fairland. At 10 miles in this morning we stopped, usually I would blast a bit further but I had crossed one of the very few bridges I would cross during the day. This one spanned the Grand Lake O The cherokees. A majestic place where every type of animal seemed to graze. We just stared at the water for a while, sweat puddled under me, I was mesmerised just by the sheer size of the lake, beautiful.

I was chased by two dogs today. While running for my life I thought to myself, we don't need performance enhancing drugs in sport, just let them get chased by a dog and you can soon up your times. Pretty sure I was running 5 minute miles while they chased me.

We arrived in Vinita quite late on. Parked in a Walmart cap park. The life of an adventurer. I will leave you tonight with a post from my younger brother. You may not have seen it. I always think to myself "don't let pain break you". This broke me.
From Luke.

I have just spoken to Sam Boatwright through the magic of FaceTime and I am now more in awe of him than ever.

For me, I just think of when I am tired and hurting. I think about how at these times the little things like perhaps the noise of insects or the heat of the sun can/could drive me insane, even at home. However, after just talking to my brother I realise how mentally tough he is, how his incredible sense of humour enables him to make everything seem trivial and how this helps him to deal with all the difficulties he is being faced with.

Sam may not be superhuman in terms of his physical attributes - he works incredibly hard to be as fit as he is - but Sam is definitely a superhuman in terms of mentality because how can you possibly prepare for the torment, the challenge, the sheer exhaustion that he faces everyday?

I do not know and probably will never know how you do it bruv but I will spend my life telling people about your achievements and making sure they know just how proud I am to share my name with you.

So people please give my brother every bit of support that you can - like his page, share his posts and most importantly donate to Help for Heroes. This man, my brother, runs for those who can't - all we have to do is help him along the way, it's not too much to ask, is it? #epicadventure #smilingbig #helpforheroes

Day 18.

A much better day. The aftermath of yesterday's run lasted well into the night. The heat was energy sapping. Something as simple as putting socks on resulted in buckets of sweat pouring from me. Last nights sleep was like jungle training without the jungle. Humid, hot and sticky. Unable to get comfortable, the entire team pretty much went without sleep. After a quick chat yesterday evening we decided the only way to beat the heat was to start as early as possible and get the mileage done early. It wasn't difficult to get up as I hadn't slept. We pressed hard out of vinita, a great little market town that reminded me a bit of home. We had stayed in a Walmart car park, it turns out this is a favourite for truckers too. The day passed without major incident, passing Chelsea, Foyil (worlds largest totem pole), claremore and Catoosa before eventually stopping in Tulsa for something to eat. It felt strange stopping for dinner and it was only 10am but the benefit of setting off early had paid off. A big bulk of the day completed before the sun hit its full strength. Only once we sat in Tulsa did I realise how far we had come from New York. I know this because in my favourite sitcom Friends, Chandler is sent there for work, they also agree, it's a long way. Tulsa was hit by a tornado a few days ago, 7 people were hospitalised from this. Today was calm, still 30 degrees but calm and peaceful.

Route 66 intertwines and cork screws the major highways. Sometimes a bridge over, others a tunnel under. It did this all the way to Edmond where we stay tonight. Tonight's RV park is amazing, such contrast to yesterday. We are parked on the banks of Arcadia Lake, a little north of Oklahoma City. My ice bath was a swim in the lake tonight with the rest of the team. The next two days are now probably going to be the toughest. A fifth team member arrives on Saturday into Oklahoma, we don't want to get too far away from him so I'm going to run two days back to back. After yesterday's horror day, I'm not looking forward to this. For those panicking about food I have added a picture of my tea. This was my pizza against helens pizza. I'm doing ok for calories. While writing this a national weather warning has just sounded out, warning us of high winds and thunderstorms. Could be an interesting night. We are so so close to the 5000 like mark now! Keep it going guys. If you have a chance and can donate please visit the website samboatwright.com this also has my live tracker on. Thanks again for all the comments, the donations, the likes just everything. #inspire #ride #beepic

Day 19.

If yesterday was a rather dull affair, today was a stark contrast. We have had a little bit of everything today. Navigation nightmares, injuries, fires, missing bridges and even a commando crawl! Today certainly lifted morale after another tortuous night of sleep. 3am this morning the public address system sounds like a nuclear war is about to happen. The RV site, silent during the night is hammered with a storm, thunder shook the RV, rain pelted us, added to this the enormous cracks of lightning. Sleep is becoming more and more rare on the RV.

When I ran in 2012 my mum managed to lose me in Montrose, Scotland. She was reading the paper as I passed, never noticing her son in the pouring rain, slogging his guts out on the pavement. A similar incident happened today. As helen and I weaved our way through Edmond towards Oklahoma City the RV seemed to lose us. It was a straight road...... yup, I know what you're thinking, how? No money, no phone and no water we pulled into a Hyundai garage. Thankfully they helped.

Once the RV had caught us up we pressed on, just as we moved a van shot passed us on fire! "The vans on fire" I shouted as Kerry who was at the back of RV at the time bolted forwards thinking I meant our RV. It seemed the driver of the truck was not that bothered. He just sat on the hard shoulder while the flames bellowed! I don't think I have ever seen anyone so calm while their truck was about to explode.

We pushed towards Bethany, a small part of Oklahoma City. Kerry had run the first section early in the morning, Helen was keeping me company at this point. As we ran we saw that there were road works ahead. We just assumed we could walk round them and that pedestrians would be fine. The bridge was actually missing. That's right, a huge section of the road was missing. The only way round was to run across the motorway! That was 8 lanes off traffic with wire fences at both sides. We found a gap. We looked down the motorway (basically the equivalent of the M1) and decided we had to sprint to the centre. We made it. Then again to the other side. One thing we had not worked out was how to get over or through the fence at the other side. We ran down the motorway for a while until at the side of the road we saw a storm drain with a tiny gap under the fence. The gap was just enough to squeeze a person under. We looked at each other, giggled, sod it. As we commando crawled up the storm drain and under the fence i couldn't help but think, 2000 miles we have come and we are crawling. We appeared to the surprise of some drivers on the streets above the motorway.

I ran fast today, whether adrenaline from the fear of being hit by traffic or just feeling good I was running great. I had 10 miles to go when my stomach cramped and my calf felt like it had a screw driver stuck in it. The mileage was dragging, my mind looked to tomorrow and all I could think about was another 50. I need sleep.

The RV park tonight is awesome, everything you could want. Great wifi. My mum has been worried so I thought I would give her a call. As I looked for somewhere to perch my ass and speak to her I sat on what can only be described as like sitting on a million tiny knives. They were lodged in my ass, little barbs! I have added a picture of my shorts. While everyone howled with laughter I was stuck! These little things were all over! Thankfully once I had stripped out of my shorts in the middle of the RV park I was able to carefully pick them out!

What a day. I've tried to show you on a map how far we have come. It doesn't fit on the screen. Running again tomorrow. Let's see what tomorrow brings. #adventure #epic #team #painintheass

Day 20.

The weather turned British today. It rained for 12 hours solid. I have noticed that everything in America is bigger, the cars, houses, farms, bugs, people and also the weather. The rain isn't just a shower, it's torrential, clothes soaking, road blocking down pours. The difference between the UK and the US is that they are prepared for it over here. Their drainage systems work pretty well. The contrast between days is huge. Yesterday we crawled up a bone dry storm drain, today there was a river flowing down the drains. The small creeks that run along the old highway were now raging torrents. The running has been good today, pain moves through my body from day to day but at the moment it's manageable. I even managed a race against Helen in the RV after 45 miles up hill. I didn't win. My last half marathon was timed at 1.57, not bad after 37 miles of hard running and rain.

Last night was the best nights sleep I've had on the RV, much cooler, probably getting ready for the early morning storms. I enjoyed running in the rain, it was a welcome change. Kerry ran the early morning miles with me before jumping in the van to watch her beloved Sheffield Wednesday. Helen ran with me for a while although her extra mileage from yesterday hurt. As Helen and I ran this morning we were met by a procession of Harley Davidsons, each one waving and pipping their horns. Brilliant. It was great to have these guys as company while the rain thundered down.

In the animated film Cars they describe the interstate as ploughing through the landscape and destroying the businesses on Route 66. It's not until you are here you see how true that is. The old highway flows with the landscape. It's dips and dives and meanders with the land. The interstate parallel to this just drives straight through the heart of the country. It's quite sad to see the boarded up buildings and fuel pumps out of service. We stopped at an old fuel pump today, braving the weather for a quick picture.

So far we have completed 1853.5 miles. I just stare at that number! It's incredible. I'm back on the bike tomorrow for the next two days. I've got to cover 300 miles in two days. We have looked at the forecast for New Mexico, 41 degrees. Wow. As we move west people seem to make more of a big deal of Route 66. We have passed a number of towns today; Hydro, Weatherford,

Clinton all of which had museums or monuments for Route 66.

Tonight we are whizzing our way back to Oklahoma City to collect the final member of our team. I know we are all ready for a fresh face to join the team.

As I run I have time to think, you could go crazy, maybe I already am. I hope to myself that even if one person is inspired to go running then I'll be a happy man. It's my hope that one student that I teach sees this and thinks, wow, i can do something amazing. I hope it makes my students and anyone reading this, to think, I need to dream big!

Day 21.

Today we crossed. We are now in Texas. We have been "shown the way to Amarillo", shocking joke I know but I'm tired. We collected the fifth member of our team last night, Darren arrived into Oklahoma just a little after 8. I could sit and watch people in an airport all day. There is never any hate in an airport, you see love and joy all the time as loved ones greet each other. It was the same for us. Helen ran and gave Darren a massive cuddle. Loved it.

It was the start of two days of cycling to catch the mileage up from the two days of running. I was not looking forward to two days on the bike at all. The roads here are not designed to spend a long time in the saddle. They go from bowling green smooth to cobbled country lane within a mile. The old highway is more a patch work of tarmac, concrete and In some areas, grass!! With all of its surface problems I still prefer it to the interstate and larger highways. My body is feeling every break in the surface, I wince and groan with pain as the bike blasts into another pothole or crack in the road. A large pothole later in the day feels like it's knocked my spine out of alignment. One of the pictures shows kerry doing some budget chiropractic work on it. We have no doctors in our team, no Physio or anything like that. Just 5 friends on a budget.

It's peaceful and quiet, bobbing along, dipping and weaving through the Texan landscape. Like most of the landscape in America it's vast, endless. Not much in between the towns, a scattering of houses here and there but generally just farm land. We passed through a few towns today, Erick, Sayre, Texola and McLean. Mclean was my favourite. Virtually abandoned, ghost town, we arrived late in the afternoon. A local lady came to talk to us. After the normal pleasantries and the bewilderment in what we are trying to do she told us of the thriving town Mclean used to be, about the antique shop she used to run. It was heart breaking to see what had happened. The town was built in 1909 by the English rancher, he tied in 1912 on the Titanic. Round the corner from where our conversation took place was a building recently demolished. She told us it was the old movie theatre, built in 1929. It was demolished yesterday. She had come into town just to look, to reminisce for a while about what the town used to be. As we said our goodbyes she asked what our favourite thing had been so far. It's simple, the people. Their kindness, generosity, smiles, faces, charity and most of all the happiness that each person seems to have. Any time I have ever done anything like this I have always been astounded by the kindness of strangers. America is no different. I have seen nothing but kindness since the day we arrived.

What a night last night was for social media! 5000 likes blasted out of the water, a share from John Bishop and my phone tells me that over 250,000 people saw last nights post!!!! Wow wow wow! Let's see what I can wake up to tomorrow.

Thank you to everyone. Sam.

#leadlegs #brokenbody #anotherday

Day 22.

It's a scorcher today! Pushed straight out of Texas this morning. A strange broken morning of riding. The head wind was brutal first thing. I decided the best thing to do was slip-stream off the RV. It worked brilliantly. Saj in the drivers seat maintaining 20mph and we blasted out of Texas, I stuck as close as I dare to the rear bumper conserving as much energy as I could for later. We called in early morning to see the Cadillac Ranch. For those not familiar this is the place where the cars look like they are planted in the ground, half the car sticks out of the earth. Tourists flock to see and spray paint their name or where they are from down the sides of the cars. The cars are randomly lodged in the ground, half way down the highway, a little ride out of Amarillo. There doesn't seem to be any rhyme or reason to this art, although I did see a huge billboard letting people know what to do if they were caught with weed. I wonder if the artist was under the influence when I the idea was born.

If you have never driven Route 66 you would be forgiven in thinking that it's a relatively easy thing to navigate. Go from Chicago to LA and follow the signs, simple? Not so much, there is probably a sign once every 100 miles, sometimes the old highway disappears completely into a dirt track. We found today that other times the old highway merges with the interstate. Our earlier run in with the law has taught us that the interstate is not an option on a bike, which means we must navigate the smaller roads.

There were not many towns on the roads today, and the few that we saw had seen better days. Ghost towns lay along this stretch of the highway, eerily overgrown homes, lifeless, in desperate need of civilisation.

The temperature maxed at 32 degrees this afternoon. I was down to just my bib shorts for riding, amazingly unattractive things. If bibs shorts are not something you know, think mid 80s wrestler or possibly what Mexican midget wrestlers wear. They are ridiculous, and as I am now finding out leave incredibly stupid tan lines. Arizona will be even hotter than this.

We had yet another storm last night. Luckily I had my thunder buddy. The storms here are biblical, end of the universe types things. Saj had gone to the shop when the storm started, he returned three hours later, everywhere closed their doors and windows. I have added a video from inside the RV.

I'm still trying fathom how I can cycle through a time zone! How crazy is that?! We are now 7 hours behind the UK. New Mexico is more like its own country, everything feels a little different. The earth here is scorched red, the rivers are the same colour. Everything looks hot, even the cows in the fields look too hot.

The team are looking forward to a running day. Two days in a sweaty RV is not good for anyone. They will get the chance to sweat with me tomorrow.

I think the only thing we can go for now is 6000 likes?! We are well on our way. You keep doing what you're doing and I'll keep doing what I'm doing. Sam

Day 23.

New Mexico is proving to be a pretty unforgiving place. There is a reason Walter White decided to cook his "product" out here. There is nothing here. Like previous days the old highway runs alongside the interstate. I counted 8 cars in 4 hours of running on the old road this morning. Weeds and grass are taking over, it won't be long before the old 66 is nothing but a grass track. I would usually list all the towns we have been through during the day, civilisation here is near non existent. Running through Tucumcari this morning you got a real sense of the desperation of these smaller towns. We set out from the campsite early, running through the town at what might be called rush hour. Everything was still, no horns tooting or people rushing to work, no suits bustling along the pavements, just lifeless. This would be the last town we saw in 50 miles of running.

The landscape here is spectacular and if for no other reason you should come just to see it. Endless mountains and burnt red cliff faces, cactai and dry arid dirt. It goes on as far as the eye can see. Any life does well to survive, the trees and plants are all fighting for those few trickles of moisture. If you are struggling to picture it, think of the surface of Mars just without any plants. At home most places are never more than 10 or 20 miles from something man-made. Whether it's a house or even just a telegraph pole. Out here it feels like you could walk for days and see nothing.

Every member of the team has run with me today. It makes a great break from the silence. We talk about anything and everything, politics to fridge magnets.

There is every insect in the world you can think of out here and I'm pretty sure they all decided to congregate for a chat on the old highway today. Every step was met with bugs scattering to avoid my trainer. All I could think of was Indiana Jones Temple of Doom when the girl has to put here hand into a dark cave filled with bugs to save Indy's life. That dark cave was my road today.

The heat here is dry, my sweat dries and turns to salt on my skin. Unlike previously where I would be saturated with sweat, my clothes stay dry. It's quite a strange feeling, and very difficult to tell when you have worked hard.

I have added the picture of my sun burn from yesterday. Today was different, factor 10,000 lathered all over. The run is painful enough without sun burn added to it.

One thing I had not taken into account when heading out here was altitude. People talk about the plains of America and the vastness of the land. Today we are in Santa Rosa. This is 5000 feet above sea level. I knew I felt like I had gone up hill more than down. Not only have we got the heat, 50 miles to run its now even harder to breath. I know at its highest it gets to 6000 feet, the optimist in me thinks, that's a lot of downhill to go. The pessimist says, the next 10 days are going to be tough.

Tomorrow night we stop in Albuquerque. Going to be a tough slog on the bike with the head wind. #epic #150 #bike #50 #run

Day 24.

A great day on the bike, feel like I haven't said that since we have been here but today was a good day. Miles passed by, helped by the breathtaking scenery. Today was all about team work. What a support team these guys have become. I drafted off the RV again today, the head wind made pedalling almost impossible. I sit about 6 inches off the back bumper, anymore and the wind hits me like a punch in the chest. At the back of the RV I'm invisible to the driver so we need clear communications between me at the back and the driver. We averaged 28mph today. For the couple of hours after dinner we stayed at an average of 30mph.

The route today has taken us through some of the most amazing places I have ever seen. What I have loved about being out here is that the landscape changes everyday. Today was green and mountainous. No red dirt or burnt rock, instead, green forest, canyons, mountains and salt flats.

We have climbed again today, up to 6300 feet, from the 5000 yesterday. All this climbing is done at 30 degree heat.

We are back to civilisation today, pushing out of Santa Rosa this morning we have passed Willard, Vaughn, Chillini, Tijeras and finally into Albuquerque. We have twice been pulled over by the police today. That takes us to a total of 11 run ins with the law. I was fearful of the law when heading here but every time they have been great. Today they were interested in what we were doing and just wanted to make sure we stayed safe. They always leave with good wishes and a handshake.

I have started to have problems with my feet, well they have been a problem for a couple of weeks but last night was the end of the line for toe nails, the pliers came out. I have attached videos and photos. You can see how my toes are actually rotting, I think it's from the rain a couple of days ago. I have taped them again to try and help them.

Albuquerque is not what I expected. After such a stunning ride into the city, through mountains and amazing forests you arrive to quite a run down edgy city. I feel slightly on edge but I can't understand why?! Just don't seem to feel quite comfortable here. The best thing about this adventure is that everyday we are somewhere different, somewhere new.

One of the best things to see today was a sign saying "high bear activity, be bear aware". We unfortunately didn't see one, or fortunately depending on whether you were on or off the RV!

Thanks again for all the likes and donations. If you are new to the page, Hello! I'm Sam and I'm very very warm. You can donate at samboatwright.com

To my friends Ella and Adam who got engaged while on holiday in America, congratulations.

#greatnews #beawesome #beepic #adventure

Day 25.

I can hand on heart say that was the toughest day of running I have ever had, in fact one of the hardest days of my life. They say to every Yong there is a yang, the balance of life. Today's torture on the road balanced out the good day I had yesterday.

We wanted to get out early this morning, 5.30am and off to Laguna from Albuquerque. The morning chill kept me cool and the miles out of Laguna were pleasant enough. After my first 7 miles I looked to the horizon and saw the mountains. Quickly scanning the landscape for the gap in them where the road might be. There was no gap. The climbs started, they never stopped. I don't know whether it's just that I don't remember the easy parts as the day was so hard but I don't remember a downhill all day. Flat, yes, occasionally but that was about my lot. The first 25 miles were gruesome, climbing up and up. Each member of the team joining me for short sections but all suffering as the air got thinner.

The climbing finally came to an end at our highest point, The Continental Divide - 7245 Feet. This is the point where water goes one way to the Pacific and the other way to the Atlantic. Tears came to my eyes as I ended today. I came so close to quitting today, I have no idea what got me through. As I saw the sign for the last half a mile kerry ran with me, it gave me the boost I needed as she told me John Bishop had just commented. I was hurting, limping and willing it to end. At the top three people donated, an Australian ex serviceman, handshake like a vice and some other bikers who had passed me on the way up.

In a morning the scenery and the landscape get me up, they get me moving. I love the changing views and breathtaking sights. That same landscape and scenery crushed me today. As i stared forward all I could think about was the mountains in front of me.

I don't know if you have ever run at altitude, I felt like a 90 year old asthmatic or possibly someone with a collapsed lung. Conversation when running was down to grunts and head nods. Although awful I am proud of myself today.

Day 26.

We have passed another state line, we are now in Arizona and wow is it hot. Today frustrated me, I will look back on today and be glad we made the decisions we made.

I pressed hard out of Gallup this morning, very hard. Average pace on the bike was 30mph, we were really shifting. The landscape was amazing and as I mentioned yesterday gives you the impetus to get up each day and go again. Starting early in the morning helps, it was 8 degrees when we departed. I drafted off the RV and we pushed on, passing Navajo Caves and big red cliffs as we sailed along. The problem with drafting off something as big as the RV is that you can't see what's coming. The roads had been fine until.... Bang! I hit a cattle grid at 32mph, this would be fine in a car, on bike the results are not great. My rear tyre exploded and dented the rim. Nearest bike repair shop, 120 miles in a small town called Show-Low. This was South of where we needed to be. Most spares I have with me, I just couldn't fit in another full wheel, so I needed a new wheel. It was 0830. We made the decision to drive South and go to the bike shop I would then peddle from there back North and pick up the original route and head to Winslow.

Bike fixed we pushed out of Show-Low. Now firmly in Arizona we had our obligatory run in with the law. Sargeant Rush was his name. He explained (in explicit) detail the laws of Arizona. Once again he was only looking out for my safety. The road was busy, cars and lorries rumbled by all day. I wasn't drafting anymore, I was up front and the RV followed me to try and give me some protection. We passed through towns, Snowflake, Taylor and Holbrook. It was 33 degrees this afternoon. It's baffling to think they have 3-4 feet of snow annually here.

Tonight we are staying just outside the town of Winslow. A Yorkshire person would describe this as "the arse end of nowhere". If Bear Grylls was here he would be out eating scorpions and drinking his own pee! We on the other hand are eating M and Ms while drinking Yorkshire Tea. Complete isolation, proper adventure.

Thanks for all the messages after yesterday's horror day. Tomorrow's forecast is even hotter. We have dropped about 1500 feet but tomorrow we climb again. Head down and crack on. #beepic #inspire #hot #arizona #adventure

Day 27.

A tough old day in Red Sands Arizona. The RV site last night could be described as "at one with nature". Not much to see but insects, rocks and tumbleweed. What it did bring us though was an amazing sunset and an even better sunrise. When people talk about the things to see before you die, the sun rising over Arizona has to be one of them.

The days here are baking hot but the nights are perishingly cold. You go to bed dripping with sweat and at some point during the night your sweat turn to icicles! I haven't experienced the point in between yet where I imagine it would be quite pleasant!

5am wake up call and we ran out of Winslow. I've always tried not to just describe pain but instead tell you how my day has been. Today my right knee hurts. It feels like it's going to collapse. I ran the first 15-20 miles this morning but had to change for the bike. I've not factored in a rest day to this challenge so instead of resting I cycled the rest of the day. The roads were pleasant and the landscape amazing.

We have climbed another 1000 feet today. I heave the air in as I pedal. I can feel my lungs pulling hard in my chest. It's relentless, I'm ready for it to be over now, we are all on countdown.

We are in Flagstaff Arizona this evening, home to a giant Meteor crater. It is amazing, I think this is where Superman came to Earth. The pictures just don't do it justice. The place, like this challenge is epic.

I know my body is getting to the point of failure now, simple mundane tasks are torture. Putting on a pair of socks, standing up and brushing your teeth are all met with a grimace and a quick shot of pain.

There are certain landmarks you look for when you're out running, at home you might run to the next lamppost or gateway. You look out for certain things in the landscape that might signal a change. For example if there is a castle you know that there is going to be a big hill! America has different markers.

1. If there are billboards on the highway we are getting close to civilisation.
2. A sea of windmills means head wind.
3. A sign saying "open range" means there is nothing for miles but the odd cow.
4. A water tower means a town.

All these things help or sometimes just make you think, oh god!

Will be another early start tomorrow. We have come over another time zone so we are now 8 hours behind the UK. #epic #run #cycle

Day 28.

I have run out of descriptive words for Arizona. It's just..... Wow. I wouldn't do it justice if I tried to describe it, you just have to come here and see it. If you do, get out of your car! On foot in the saddle on flipping horse back if you want, however you see this great state, breath it in, take in everything it's got because it is fantastic.

On the way to RV site last night I turned to the team and said, "guys, it's pointless coming all this way to not see the Grand Canyon? It's only 80 miles North of here, I can do that and then blast into the afternoon and keep up. What do you think?" The answer was a resounding, hell yeah I want to see it. If you want something to add to your bucket list, try this. Stay in Flagstaff Arizona, get up at 5am and get on your bike. Head North on the 89 towards Cameron. It's stunning. The first climb is 1000 feet which takes you from the 7000 feet at Flagstaff up to 8000 feet but once you have climbed it's either downhill or flat and it's breathtaking on a whole new scale. Get down to 5000 feet then climb again up to 7000 feet at the South Rim of the canyon. I can't put the Canyon into words. Grand for something as spectacular as that just doesn't come close. I could stare at it all day. Every angle you see something new, a trail, a cave, the river or a new rock formation.

We pressed hard away from the Canyon passing, mountain lions, elk, deer and coyotes. A deer ran parallel to me this morning. Effortlessly keeping up, camply prancing its way through the grass and over the fences. I have added the pics of my garmin speedo from two of my rides today. You get the idea of average page or distance covered. I aim to cover 50-55 miles in 2 hours on the bike.

We have seen the first road sign for Los Angeles. We are just less than 400 miles away. I love telling people how far we have come and what I do everyday. To put what I've done today into perspective.... if you live in Skipton, like me. Birmingham is 140 miles away. Yup, it's a long long way. If my maths is right, we have 4 days to go!

As a team we have talked about high and low points. Dropping the other two members back at the airport was a massive low. We have missed them. Today was just a huge huge high point. 150 miles in 6 hours and seeing one of Earths greatest natural attractions. What a brilliant day.

For those out there that think it's nice and pleasant. Pain is constant but at this point it's not going to change. I have attached a picture of a toenail I pulled out after this mornings session. It was feeling lose, unfortunately that little fella could not make the entire trip. #epic #adventure #highpoint

Day 29.

Arizona has given me everything it's got, it's beaten me to my knees, but we have made it to California. I'll never forget Arizona, the heat, mountains, lakes and lizards have been out of this world. What a unit the team have been today. Kerry led me out over the first

10k, pushing out of Kingman aiming for Oatman. Last night the sky was a dark red, "pink sky at night Shepard's delight", the saying goes, not in America. We were met with rain this morning as we pushed out, although it wasn't massively unpleasant, it's more like a luke warm shower. It persisted most of the morning as we tracked the 66 alongside the interstate. After 8 miles the old road swings under the interstate and starts to move towards Oatman on the originally named, Oatman Road. As we plodded along the road I could see the mountains off in the distance. We were in a basin so I knew at some point we were going over. A long straight road led to the foot of the mountains. The eclipse came and went, nothing much to see due to the heavy thunderstorm clouds sitting over us.

Helen ran with me as we progressed along the straight road towards the mountains, after a few miles Saj joined us, we all sweated together. At the foot of the climb the team went back in the RV. Darren came out and we attacked the mountain. In perfect military time we plodded, left, right, left right..... punching up the hill we moved. It started off gradual, we joked, maybe it's an optical illusion and not really that steep. Our joke was short lived, the mountains gradual gradient turned very steep very fast. I knew it was steep as it went upon bends, the next corner snaking back way up the mountain above our heads. Motorcyclists passed us a mile up the climb, 25 minutes later I could still see them climbing up towards the summit. I love to look at the faces on the people that pass me, some take photos, some smile and others cheers and peep their horns.

As Darren hit his 6 mile, he had hit the limit. Helen came out again as did Saj, kerry whooped and cheered from the van as the punishing heat and 3000 foot climb took its toll on my body. 30 miles done, 3000 feet climbed and my body was screaming but we were at the top.

We entered Oatman at lunch time. Oatman is sold in the guide book as a ghost town. So we were a little surprised to see a town of hustle and bustle. A selling point for the town was the wild donkeys. A very strange site to see. I can't understand why there are not more towns along the 66 that sell themselves as "Ghost Towns". We have certainly been to many towns that were more isolated than Oatman. Oatmans other claim to fame was the fact the Clark Gable and Carole Lombard spent their honeymoon in the towns hotel, it's still set up exactly the same as it was then.

We pushed out of Oatman after dinner and pressed towards Needles. It was warm and only getting hotter. I passed a sign for a town called bullhead city, it helped me reminisce about my childhood spent catching bullheads at Beck Hall in Malham. The daydream allowed me to drift along for a few miles.

I wave at all the drivers that pass, some wave, some smile, those that do nothing are still given a smile but as they pass it's usually met with a four letter expletive. One driver passed today, "you ok?" He asks, my mind is saying, "hell no, do I look ok? Please take me home, get me a cold drink and let me sleep for the next 3 days!" Unfortunately I give the standard "yup, I'm good, cheers pal". I press on, as i do a Dodge Challenger passes me and swiftly climbs the hill in front of me and disappears into the haze of heat. I curse myself, "that's why they invented the motor car you flipping dickhead". I plod on.

We crossed a bridge tonight and the state line was in the middle of the river, we are in our last state for the adventure. We are close. As we enter California the palm trees have started, I can tell just by the smell we are some where different. The palm trees have a certain smell, the landscape has changed slightly.

Back on the bike tomorrow. So close now I can feel it. If you can help me get to 6000! Let's go people, let's see what you've got! #6000likes #imsweating #runhard #cyclehard #epic

Day 30.

Sometimes I astound myself at my own stupidity, why the hell did I think about the finish? Why allow complacency to come in. You complete twonk! It's wasn't painful, my legs are not broken today my mind started to make me think I was done, I screamed at the Tarmac, yelled at anything and everything but really I was mad at myself. Today was harder, heat, exhaustion, the roads it felt like the universe was sending me one hell of a test.

Pushing out of Needles this morning after what felt like a 3 minute sleep last night, we left with sunrise. The heat at this point was quite balmy, pleasant you might even say. The old road seemed not to bad and off we went. After about 15 minutes the undulating terrain started to get to me, I just couldn't find a rhythm, no gear seemed to be the right one to sit at a decent cadence, it was plain and simple hard work. After 30 minutes I could feel my body searching for energy, I had done everything the same as the previous 29 days, something was different. I was empty. Yesterday had taken much more out of me than I had thought, it felt like my body was eating itself. An hour passed and I started to see dots, it was time to refuel. I knelt on the road, urgh, was the only think I felt.

The second hour improved, pace was averaging 26mph and I felt strong again. The dessert is a strange place, dry (obviously) but also quite serene and spectacular at the same time. The train line carves through the dessert, huge trains with an endless amount of carriages barrage their way across the country. I knew of the road was near the train line it would be relatively flat. The old road goes from bowling green smooth to rugged edgy canal path tarmac within seconds, which when moving at 30mph, hurts.

We passed a few towns today, probably the most famous was Hinkley, made famous by the film Erin Brokovich. Needless to say we didn't stop for a drink of water. The temperature today was 39 degrees, that's hot. Very hot. I see now why the Tour De France riders are so small, its nothing to do with pace, it's so their bodies don't act like a massive solar panel. At 6'3 and one of the palest men alive the sun is not my friend.

We broke the day into 1 hour stints just so I could rehydrate. I tried to carry my water on the bike but when I went to drink it, it was boiling. Not particularly refreshing. Usually when I get back on the RV at end of the day I have a cold shower. Even the cold water on the RV is hot.

Today was my last full day on the bike. It feels great knowing I don't have to cycle 150 miles again. Today was tough, very tough. I never thought the heat was this bad. I can only describe it as cycling in an oven, the air im pulling in as warm stagnant air. There is no relief from the heat. Let's see what tomorrow brings.

We have nearly got to 5500 like so let's try push 6000. We have made it to £3000 on the donations. Brilliant guys. Thank you. Sam.

#hot #sweat. #bike #route66

Day 31.

We are into double digits, what a brilliant thing to be able to write. I can almost feel the ocean on my feet. The rain of New York seems like a life time ago. 3000 miles and we are almost there. I feel like I should write something motivational and inspiring but words are failing me, whether it's fatigue or just knowing I'm so close, I'm exhausted.

We spent our penultimate night on the RV in a small campsite in Victorville. A beautiful little site, we had a BBQ and sat in the sun. We watched as rabbits and squirrels hurried around the site. Considering how hot the day had been the temperatures did drop to something almost bearable.

I look back and think of everything we have come through, the states, landscapes, towns and cities. I look at how different each day has been. How the people have changed, the waves, the accents even the buildings. I will miss telling the different people what I'm doing and looking at their reactions. You can see the cogs moving as they try and work out what I've just said to them. That's right, 50 mile run and 150 mile cycle. It's been met with a number of different responses, generally "wow", "dude, you rock" or the most common "sh*t thats a long way". All of the responses are met with a little grin and a "yup, it's a flipping long way".

If you were thinking about coming out here and you had any reasons not to, just come for the people. The people are what has made this trip amazing. There are 326 million people in America, I have only encountered 3 idiots. That's a pretty good ratio.

Out of Victorville this morning was a tough run. As has become our routine, kerry led me out. We were straight into climbs. The town certainly has some interesting inhabitants! We met a few of them, one guy was cycling with a fridge on the front of his bike! They were probably wondering what these two runners were doing before sunrise charging up the Main Street. As kerry jumped back on the RV, Helen came to run. It was more like trail running while Helen was with me. The pavement gave way to gravel tracks down the side of the highway, not ideal. We made good progress out of the town onto the quieter roads. Darren joined us as we continued on towards LA. At the height of today's climb we went up to 4000 feet. The climb was hard and so going but coming down made the hard work worth while. We descended most of the afternoon making great time, Darren managing a half marathon.

We entered the suburbs of LA, the smog over the downtown area obvious from a far. We ran through Fontana and into Pomona, a leafy little suburb with a very nice campsite. Tonight will be our last night on the RV. In some ways I'll miss it. I'm sure on the weeks and months to come I'll look back and think about it a lot. Right now I just want a normal bed, not one that rocks when a mouse farts! I want to be able to walk around without banging my head.

Tomorrow I will run on to Santa Monica Pier and finish. I aiming to finish at 1pm here or 9pm back home. It will hopefully be live so check it out if you can.

Thanks to everyone that has liked/shared/donated or anything that has made me smile. One more time people. Let's give it a push! #6000

Day 32.

Well, that was emotional. What a day, what a month... in fact what a year it has been. I'm laid on my hotel bed writing this. Yes, I'm not on wheels, I can stretch my legs out and my toes are not in a draw, I can go to the toilet without waking the rest of the team as the whole RV shakes when you move, I can stand up straight but mainly I can just lay down.

I have just run across a continent. Just over 3000 miles has been covered, 2 stone in weight has come off me, but so many memories made. We sat and had our last meal together on the RV last night and reminisced about the different things we had remembered. We started talking about new challenges and what we could accomplish. I do believe this team could do great things, from the guys with us at the start to those that ended they have been amazing. Without each one of them I would never have made it.

This morning as i cycled I wondered how anyone in LA commutes on a bike? I absolutely crapped myself for about two hours. Cars whizzed passed me, cracks appeared from nowhere in the road, crazy people also on bikes who looked like Uncle Albert from Only Fools and Horses come up next to you at traffic lights. I wanted to get myself into a position where I was 20 miles out, then I would run, Darren would pedal next to me and carry water, the rest of the team dropped the RV off and headed to the finish line.

The running was good, my calf has been a problem over the last couple of days but that wasn't stopping me this morning. The other reason I was. It stopping was fearing for my life as we ran through some of the not so touristy areas of LA. The smells, sites and sounds of downtown LA were every bit of randomness that this adventure has been all about. As we stopped for a drink Darren said, it's not hours and miles and miles anymore Sam. You are minutes and single digits away. I couldn't say anything. I just smiled. Single sodding digits. Brilliant.

We pushed again and aimed for Colorado Avenue, Darren pedalled ahead to Santa Monica Pier for the finish line and the end of the mother road. I ran, stronger and faster as the adrenaline pumped. I think if anyone had spoken to me at this point I would have just cried, I was an emotional wreck. I could see the Santa Monica Pier archway sign. I crested the tiny bridge, jumped the fence to avoid the people and ran down the bridge and onto the pier. I could hear the team shouting and clapping. As they did the rest of the pier around them joined in. I had made it. I had run and cycled coast to coast. We had navigated the mother road and we had finished.

I'm sure tomorrow I will feel a little lost but for now all I can do is lay here and smile about what the team and I have achieved. I couldn't have done it without them. Thank you to you all. Kerry Germany Darren Foster, Helen Foster, Mustafa Hussain, Matthew Wright and Anthony Hannan.

Thank you to every single person that has liked my pages, for the donations that stand now at nearly £5000, for every comment, message and email. I may never get chance to say it in person but these are what has kept me going.

To anyone out there dreaming of an adventure. Just go. You only live once. Do what ever you can to make another person smile. I will write a book about this adventure as I did my last so please stay tuned.......

For me, my next adventure starts in 5 days and I cannot wait. I get married.

So, for me, I bid you good night. America, thanks for the memories. Sam

The route we planned

Date	Day	From	To	Miles	Run/ Cycle	Rest Areas	Notes
24/7	1	New York -Times Square	Philadelphia	97	Cycle/ Run	X	Towns/ villages
25/7	2	Philadelphia	Washington DC	139	Run/ Cycle	4	
26/7	3	Washington DC	Hagerstown (RA just before)	50	Run	X	
27/7	4	Hagerstown	Washington	150	Cycle	5	Towns/ Villages
28/7	5	Washington	Pittsburgh	50	Run	1	
29/7	6	Pittsburgh	Columbus	150	Cycle	7	Matty & Hannan Go Home ☹
30/7	7	Columbus	Wilmington	50	Run	1	
31/7	8	Wilmington	Greensburg	150	Cycle	2	Via Cincinnati (see Sam's Friend)
1/8	9	Greensburg	Indianapolis	50	Run	x	Towns/ Villages
2/8	10	Indianapolis	Chicago	150	Cycle	3	
3/8	11	Chicago	Run 50, then drive to rest area in-between Pontac & Chenona approx. 25miles	50	Run	X	

4/8	12	Rest area in-between Pontac & Chenona	Gateway Arch rest area	150	Cycle	3	
5/8	13	Gateway Arch rest area	Run 50, then drive to next rest area just after Union approx. 10miles	50	Run	X	
6/8	14	Rest area after Union	Springfield	150	Cycle	2	
7/8	15	Springfield	Run 50, then drive to rest area @ Joplin approx. 20 miles	50	Run	1	
8/8	16	Joplin	Rest Area after Bristow approx. 20 miles	150	Cycle	2	
9/8	17	Rest Area after Bristow	Bethany	50	Run	1	
10/8	18	Bethany	Shamrock	150	Cycle	1	Lots of towns/ villages
11/8	19	Shamrock	Run 50, then drive approx. 15miles to next rest area before Amarillo	50	Run	1	
12/8	20	Rest Area before Amarillo	Rest Area after Tucumcari	150	Cycle	1	Darren Arrives!! ☺
13/8	21	Rest Area after Tucumcari	Rest Area after Santa Rosa	50	Run	X	Village
14/8	22	Rest Area after Santa Rosa	Grants	150	Cycle	1	Towns/ Villages
15/8	23	Grants	Gallup	50	Run	X	

16/8	24	Gallup	Rest Area after Winslow (Near Meteor Crater)	150	Cycle	3	Towns/ Villages
17/8	25	Rest Area after Winslow (Near Meteor Crater)	Rest Area after Flagstaff (Humphreys peak)	50	Run	X	
18/8	26	Rest Area after Flagstaff (Humphreys peak)	Rest Area after Kingman	150	Cycle	1	Towns/ Villages
19/8	27	Rest Area after Kingman	Fenner	50	Run	X	Towns/ Villages
20/8	28	Fenner	Hesperia	150	Cycle	2	Towns/ Villages
21/8	29	Hesperia	Ontario	50	Run	X	Towns/ Villages
22/8	30	Ontario	LA – STANA MONICA PIER FINISH LINE	50-70?	Cycle	X	Towns/ Villages

The route I actually took

Date	Day	From	To	Miles Completed	Run/ Cycle	Where We Stayed
24/7	1	New York -Times Square	Philadelphia	97	Cycle/ Run	Carpark
25/7	2	Philadelphia	Washington DC	139	Cycle	Campsite
26/7	3	Washington DC	Hagerstown (RA just before)	50	Run	Campsite Yogi Bear
27/7	4	Hagerstown	Uniontown	150	Cycle	KOA (America Campsite)
28/7	5	Uniontown	Pittsburgh	50	Run	Peg & John's Street
29/7	6	Pittsburgh	Columbus (Blacklick)	150	Cycle	Carpark
30/7	7	Columbus (Blacklick)	Loveland	50	Run	Sion & Shelly's
31/7	8	Loveland	Greensburg (Batesville)	150	Cycle	KOA
1/8	9	Greensburg (Batesville)	Indianapolis	50	Run	KOA
2/8	10	Indianapolis	Chicago	150	Cycle	Hotel – Kindly gifted by Sion & Shelly
3/8	11	Chicago	Cornell	50	Run	Campsite - Fred
4/8	12	Cornell	Springfield	105	Cycle	KOA
5/8	13	Springfield	St Louis	62.5	Run	KOA

6/8	14	St Louis	Doolittle	150	Cycle	Truck stop
7/8	15	Doolittle	Strafford	50	Run	Campsite
8/8	16	Stafford	Joplin	100	Cycle	RV carpark
9/8	17	Joplin	Vinta	50	Run	Walmart carpark
10/8	18	Vinta	Edmond	150	Cycle	Arcada lake campsite
11/8	19	Edmond	El reno	50	Run	KOA
12/8	20	El Reno	Clinton	50	Run	Carpark next to train track
13/8	21	Clinton	Mclean – had to drive to Amarillo due to no roads apart from interstate	130	Cycle	Ranch RV park
14/8	22	Amarillo	Tucumcari	80	Cycle	KOA
15/8	23	Tucumcari	Santa Rosa	50	Run	RV park
16/8	24	Santa Rosa	Albuquerque	152	Cycle	RV park
17/8	25	Albuquerque	Gallup	50	Run	USA RV park
18/8	26	Gallup	Winsolm	86	Cycle	Holomovi State Park
19/8	27	Winsolm	Flagstaff	52	Run	RV park
20/8	28	Flagstaff	Kingman	150	Cycle	KOA
21/8	29	Kingman	Needles	50	Run	Desert View RV park
22/8	30	Needles	Victorvilla	133	Cycle	Shady Oasis
23/8	31	Victorvilla	Pomona	31	Run	KOA
24/8	32	Pomona	St Monica Pier	70	Cycle/Run	Hotel Hermosa